The Last Great Gold Rush

A Klondike Reader

The Last Great Gold Rush
A Klondike Reader

Edited by Graham Wilson

Wolf Creek Books
Whitehorse, Yukon

Canadian Cataloguing in Publication Data
Graham Wilson, Editor
The Last Great Gold Rush:
A Klondike Reader

ISBN 0-9687091-2-5

Copy Editing by Clélie Rich,
  Rich Words Editing Services,
  Vancouver, BC.
Design and Production by
  Wolf Creek Books Inc.
Printed and Bound in Canada
  by Friesens Printers, Altona,
  Manitoba.

This book is dedicated to my favorite stampeders — Lauren, Emily and Jessica.
G.W.

**WOLF CREEK
BOOKS INC**
Box 31275,
Whitehorse, Yukon
Y1A 5P7
info@wolfcreek.ca
www.wolfcreek.ca

Contents

The Creeks

Paris of the North

Exodus

Acknowledgements

"The Men That Don't Fit In," "The Spell of the Yukon," "The Cremation of Sam McGee," "The Shooting of Dan McGrew," "The Law of the Yukon," by Robert Service, from *Songs of a Sourdough*, 1907.

"The Outfit Of An Argonaut," by Ernest Ingersoll, from *Gold Fields of the Klondike*, 1897.

"The Saloon In Skagway," "Sheep Camp Washed Away," "Saloons," by Tappan Adney, from *The Klondike Stampede*, 1900.

"Approaching Chilkoot Pass," "The Chilkoot Pass," by Margaret Shand, from *The Summit and Beyond*.

"Miles Cañon," "Clarence J. Berry and Wife," by John W. Leonard, from *The Gold Fields of the Klondike*, 1897.

"The Grand Cañon of the Yukon," by Frederick Schwatka, from *Report of a Military Reconnaissance in Alaska, Made in 1883*, 1885.

"A Dangerous Voyage," "Exodus," by William B. Haskell, from *Two Years in the Klondike and Alaskan Gold Fields, 1896-1898*, 1898.

"To Build a Fire," "The One Thousand Dozen," by Jack London, from *The Complete Stories of Jack London*, 1910.

"Methods of Mining," by William Ogilvie, from *Early Days on the Yukon*, 1913.

"A Woman Pioneer in the Klondike and Alaska," by Emma Kelly.

"Dawson in the Midst of the Boom," "Exodus," by Arthur T. Walden, from *A Dog Puncher on the Yukon*, 1928.

"From Dawson to the Sea," by Jack London, from *The Buffalo Express*, June 4, 1899.

"Disaster at Nome," by Rex Beach, from *Personal Exposures*, 1940.

Introduction

The Klondike Gold Rush was the last great gold rush. It was a spectacular adventure that caught the attention of the world. Tens of thousands of people made the journey north. Their pursuit was gold, and they risked everything to reach Dawson City.

The echo of the gold rush can be felt to this day. The Chilkoot Trail, White Pass and Yukon Route Railway, and false front buildings of Skagway and Dawson City are reminders of events a hundred years ago. When you visit the beaches of Dyea in November and feel the icy rain on your cheeks you empathize with the stampeders. To stand at the summit of the Chilkoot Pass in spring and see snowfields threatening to avalanche is humbling. The Yukon River with its turbulent and frigid waters still intimidates canoeists. Echoes of the Klondike Gold Rush reverberate in Alaska and the Yukon and perhaps always will.

The Klondike Gold Rush was fueled by greed, desperation and ignorance. The stampeders endured unimaginable hardships and took great risks. Some were killed by the trail and others traumatized by the rigors of the ordeal. The vast majority left broke. Most experienced the adventure of a lifetime and told their stories thousands of times back home to anyone who would listen. In many ways the greatest riches to come from the Klondike valley were its stories.

The accounts in this collection illustrate many perspectives of the stampeders. They tell a passionate and haunting story. First-hand accounts are not always historically reliable although the contradictions and exaggerations in these writings are revealing and these pieces capture the spirit of the stampede. Sometimes the most outrageous stories have an absurd tendency to be the most historically accurate. The blurring of fact and fiction is understandable considering the nature of the Klondike Gold Rush.

Some of the stampeders were professional writers who were sent to the Klondike by magazines and newspapers. Perhaps the greatest chronicler was Tappan Adney, who wrote for Harper's Illustrated Weekly. Adney's accounts are insightful and written in an accessible style. William Ogilvie was the first surveyor of the Yukon and his books capture the mining history in a way other writers could not. Arthur T. Walden portrays the rigors of dog mushing although he is known for exaggerating details. All these writers have captured different elements of the gold rush. They provide important insights and tell fascinating stories.

Unfortunately these stories tend to only record the experiences of the stampeders. The contribution and participation of First Nations people to the Klondike Gold Rush is minimized and often not credited. Derisive descriptions and racist comments abound in journals and published accounts from this period. With this in mind contemporary readers must appreciate that only a partial story is being told in this collection.

In a similar vein the contribution of women to the Klondike Gold Rush is also distorted. While some women worked as prostitutes or dance hall entertainers, most women had more conventional occupations such as shop workers, cooks or teachers. Some women established important businesses, which they eventually parlayed into mine ownership. Many of the most successful people to reach Dawson City were women.

By carefully reading the stampeders' accounts we can gain insights into the last great gold rush. As Robert Service wrote "There were strange things done in the midnight sun." In many ways, however, we have an incomplete understanding of what really happened during the Klondike Gold Rush and much mystery remains.

Bonanza!

When the small steamship Excelsior docked in San Francisco in July 1897, the world was watching. Aboard this vessel were millionaires who had been penniless men only months before. As these scruffy miners swaggered down the gangplank carrying jars, satchels and cases filled with gold, more than five thousand people crowded the docks and cheered.

A few days later the steamship Portland landed at Seattle with sixty-eight miners and almost a ton of gold. The news of the find grabbed newspaper headlines and was on everyone's lips. Overnight, the word Klondike took on mythic proportions.

Within days thousands flocked to west coast towns from San Francisco to Vancouver trying to book passage north. The fact that the Klondike was more than fifteen hundred miles away and over a precipitous mountain pass would not deter many. Gold fever had grasped the nation, and everyone wanted the chance to try their luck in the new frontier.

The 1890s was a period of economic depression. Bread lines were long and opportunities few. These were fertile conditions for a gold rush. The Klondike was the hope of relief during a time of worldwide despair and difficulty. The stampede north was an opportunity for the ordinary person and was never exclusively for experienced miners. Fueled by doctors, plumbers, clerks, the poor, the rich, it was everyone's gold rush. Just about anyone could be a stampeder.

In the frenzy to move this throng to Alaska, ships were brought in from everywhere. These ships were filled far beyond their capacity in the enthusiasm to reach Alaska. When not enough ships could be found, the most rickety, worn-out vessels were spirited from the bone-yards. The gold would not wait, and stampeders would pay everything they had for passage.

Each miner needed almost a ton of supplies — enough to last a year. Everything from dehydrated vegetables to collapsible boats was sold. Warehouses of dried meat, beans and flour were emptied; their contents sometimes auctioned to the highest bidder. The free flow of money and the unimaginable demand for goods attracted a frenzy of suppliers. Since many of the stampeders were inexperienced in both mining and the outdoors, this was also an opportunity for the unscrupulous. Many arrived in Alaska ill-equipped for the northern environment.

As the wealthy veterans of the Klondike bought rounds of drinks in the bars of San Francisco and Seattle, thousands planned their passage to the gold fields. The rush was on. A gold rush like no other.

The Men That Don't Fit In
Robert Service

There's a race of men that don't fit in,
   A race that can't stay still;
So they break the hearts of kith and kin,
   And they roam the world at will.
They range the field and they rove the flood,
   And they climb the mountain's crest.
Theirs is the curse of the gypsy blood,
   And they don't know how to rest.

If they just went straight, they might go far;
   They are strong and brave and true;
But they're always tired of the things that are,
   And they want the strange and new.
They say: "Could I find my proper groove,
   What a deep mark I would make!"
So they chop and change, and each fresh move
   Is only a fresh mistake.
And each forgets, as he strips and runs
   With a brilliant, fitful pace,
It's the steady, quiet, plodding ones
   Who win in the lifelong race.
And each forgets that his youth has fled,
   Forgets that his prime is past,
Till he stands one day, with a hope that's dead,
   In the glare of the truth at last.

He has failed, he has failed;
    he has missed his chance;
   He has just done things by half.
Life's been a jolly good joke on him,
   And now is the time to laugh.

Ha, ha! He is one of the Legion Lost;
    He was never meant to win.
He's a rolling stone, and it's bred in the bone;
    He's a man who won't fit in.

The Outfit Of An Argonaut
Ernest Ingersoll

To be well prepared is half the battle. This is the substance of an old adage which is peculiarly adapted to the case of one starting out to the Alaska or Yukon gold fields in the search of wealth, or even of a simple livelihood. The conditions of life in any newly discovered mining country are such as to place a man on his mettle, to bring out everything that is in him to make him resourceful and self-reliant. But these things being equal, it is the one who has just the right equipment who will have the advantage when the going is hard and to all appearances pretty even.

To be sober, strong, and healthy is the first requisite for any one who wants to battle successfully for a year or two in the frozen lands of the far North. A physique hardy enough to withstand the most rigorous climate is an absolute necessity. With a temperature varying from almost 100° above zero in midsummer to 50°, 60°, and even 70° below that point in winter, with weeks of foggy, damp, thawing weather, and with winds that rage at times with the violence of hurricanes, the man with a weak constitution is bound to suffer untold hardship. No one with weak lungs or subject to rheumatism ought to think of wintering along the Yukon. In short, making the venture means, according to one who has tried it, "packing provisions over pathless mountains, towing a heavy boat against a five to eight-mile current, over battered boulders, digging in the bottomless frost, sleeping where night overtakes, fighting gnats and mosquitoes by the millions, shooting seething canyons and rapids and enduring for seven long months a relentless cold which never rises above zero and frequently falls to 80° below."

If a man is able to meet these conditions he is almost sure of making a good living and takes chances with the rest in making a fortune. It is not alone to the physical side of the question that one should look. Temperament counts for a great deal in the miner's life. Men should be of cheerful, hopeful dispositions and willing workers. Those of sullen, morose natures, although they may be good workers, are very apt, as soon as the novelty of the country wears off, to become dissatisfied, pessimistic, and melancholy.

Good judgment is also a prime requisite. Once in the atmosphere of the gold country one hears constantly of newly found placers which are reported to be vastly richer than anything yet discovered. With each such report scores of miners leave diggings which are vastly superior to those which they propose to seek six, 20, or 100 miles away. If one is constantly on the jump from claim to claim there is evidently no time left for the only work that counts, separating the gold from its containing earths. One of the returning miners on the *Excelsior* said that the hardest work he had to do in the Klondike region was to keep pegging away at his claim, which, by the way, was a very good one, and give a deaf ear to the stories of fabulous wealth being found just beyond the nearest range of mountains. These stories are often put in circulation by people who are anxious to see certain claims forsaken by their owners that they themselves may step in and become the owners.

As to the outfit, both that part of it which bears on the journey proper and those things which are to form the basis of existence for the stay in the gold country, the greatest care must be exercised. To meet with the largest measure of success and in order to be in a position to move and work rapidly, which amounts to the same thing, one must strike a happy medium between taking too much and leaving behind some of the numerous essentials. Joseph Ladue, who has spent years in this country and who is given credit for having founded Dawson City, says in regard to this:

"It is a great mistake to take anything except what is necessary. The trip is a long, arduous one, and a man should not add one pound of baggage to his outfit that can be dispensed with. I have known men who loaded themselves up with rifles, revolvers, and shotguns. This is entirely unnecessary. Revolvers will get you into trouble, and there is no use of taking them with you, as large game of any character is rarely found on the trip. I have prospected through this region for some years and have only seen one moose. You will not see any large game whatever on your trip from Juneau to Dawson City, therefore do not take any firearms along."

In addition to the great inconvenience of carrying a great deal of luggage, it is a matter of continual expense. It is said that the Indians are disposed to gauge a man's ability to pay by the amount of baggage he takes with him, and scale their prices accordingly. At 15, 20, or 25 cents a pound for packing over the Chilkoot Pass it makes considerable difference whether a man has with him a hundred-weight or half a ton of freight. Then there are steamer charges, wharfage fees, and often portage expenses to be defrayed, to say nothing of customs duties. One hundred and fifty pounds of baggage is all that is allowed for a passenger on the Yukon River boats and those sailing from Seattle and San Francisco for Alaskan ports. The general practice as to clothing for miners who remain over winter is to adopt the dress of the natives. Water boots are made of seal or walrus skins; dry weather, or winter boots, from various skins, fur trimmed. Trousers are made of Siberian fawn and marmot skins, while the upper garment, combined with a hood, called parka, is made of marmot trimmed with long fur, which helps to protect the face of the person wearing it. Flannels can be worn under these and not be any heavier than clothing worn in a country with zero weather. For bedding, woolen blankets are used, combined with fur robes. If the former are used it is well to be provided with two pairs. The best robes are of wolf skin, but they cost $100 apiece. There are cheaper ones made of bear, mink, and fox skins. A good, stout pair of rubber boots is essential. The boots made by the natives sell from $2 to $5 a pair.

As to provisions, it is impossible to lay down any definite scheme. The first consideration is to have enough to last for the journey from the coast to the interior. Figuring on 30 days as the shortest time possible in which this trip can be made, the supply ought to be about as follows: 20 pounds of flour, 12 pounds of bacon, 12 pounds of beans, four pounds of butter, five pounds of vegetables, five pounds of dried fruits, four cans of condensed milk, five pounds of sugar, one pound of tea, three pounds of coffee, one and one half pounds of salt, five pounds of corn-meal, a small portion of pepper and mustard, and baking-powder.

To one accustomed to camp life there are many things in the way of utensils and apparatus generally that can be dispensed with which, to the man new to such modes of living, are, or seem to be, absolutely necessary. A pretty complete outfit includes matches, cooking utensils and dishes, frying pan, water kettle, duck tent, rubber blanket, bean pot, drinking-cup, two plates, teapot, knife and fork, large and small cooking pans. A fine addition to the culinary department will be a good assortment of fishhooks, gill nets, and fishing tackle. These ought to be graded through the medium and small sizes. Northern fish are for the most party gamey.

Ample provision must be made for the boat, raft, and sled construction, which is a feature of every journey overland. To this end these items will be found not only useful but absolutely necessary: One jack-plane, one whip saw, one cross-cut saw, one rip-saw, one axe, one hatchet, one hunting-knife, one two-foot rule, six pounds of assorted nails, three pounds of oakum, five pounds of pitch, 150 feet of rope.

Inasmuch as gnats and mosquitoes abound all over the Yukon interior, some means of protection from their assaults must be provided. Mosquito netting is recommended, and it is well to buy that with the smallest mesh obtainable. Snow spectacles and a simple medicine chest ought to find a place in every outfit. One man ought never to try the trip alone, and where four or five pool their interests one tent, one stove and one set of tools will suffice for the party.

After the supplies for the trip to the mines have been decided upon, the more extensive task of laying in provisions for the stay can be taken up. A good, safe rule is to estimate on remaining on the Yukon a full year. If one decides later to prolong the time it will be easier to send back or go back to Juneau for further supplies than to be burdened with them during the first months of life in camp, and more especially when making the first trip over the mountains. As a general rule miners find it to best advantage to buy the larger part of their outfits in Juneau rather than in the United States or in the Yukon. Buying in the United States one has to pay the freight to Juneau or Skagway, and perhaps wharfage at those points. The prices prevailing in Juneau for the necessary commodities are not prohibitory at all. But the same cannot be said of the tariff in vogue among the storekeepers of Dawson City, as witness the following scale of prices: Flour, per 100 lbs., $12; moose ham, per lb., $1; caribou meat, per lb., 65 cents; beans, per lb., 10 cents; rice, per lb., 25 cents; sugar, per lb., 25 cents; bacon, per lb., 40 cents; butter, per roll, $1.50; eggs, per doz., $1.50; better eggs, per doz., $2; salmon, each, $1 to $1.50; potatoes, per lb., 25 cents; turnips, per lb., 15 cents; tea, per lb., $1; coffee, per lb. 50 cents; dried fruits, per lb., 35 cents; canned fruits, 50 cents; canned meats, 75 cents; lemons, each, 20 cents; oranges, each, 50 cents; tobacco, per lb., $1.50; liquors, per drink, 50 cents; shovels, $2.50; picks, $5; coal oil, per gallon, $1; overalls, $1.50; underwear, per suit, $5 to $7.50; shoes, $5; rubber boots, $10 to $15; lumber, per 1,000 feet, $150.

In some of the camps further back from the river even higher prices prevail. Some idea of them can be gained from the following: Bacon, per lb., 75 cents; coffee, per lb., $1; sugar, per lb., 50 cents; eggs, per doz., $2; condensed milk, per can, $1; picks, each $15; shovels, each, $15.

Of course, a few months will make a great difference in these matters. Already the steamboat companies doing business on the Yukon are making plans to send thousands of tons of food supplies and clothing to the gold field when the ice breaks up next summer. Their efforts will be largely supplemented by private enterprises of one kind or another, so that it is confidently expected that the exorbitant rates which now exist on the Klondike will be materially reduced next summer.

A good clothing outfit for a year's stay consists of: Two pairs heaviest wool socks, one pair Canadian laragans or shoe packs, one pair German socks, two pairs heaviest woolen blankets, one oil blanket or canvas, one mackinaw suit, two heavy flannel shirts, two pairs heavy overalls, two suits heavy woolen underwear, one pair rubber boots (crack-proof preferable), one pair snowshoes, heavy cap and fleece-lined mittens. To the prosperous mechanic or businessman this list may look a little scant as to some of its numbers. For the enlightenment of those who would be thus critical be it said that it is the custom among miners to resort to frequent washings and mendings rather than to carry along a great variety and large number of the various articles of apparel.

The situation in Alaska as regards the collection of customs duties is, to say the least, a little complicated at the present moment. Acting under orders from Secretary Gage, the newly appointed collector for the territory, Mr. Ivey of Oregon has established a sub-port of entry at Dyea. Of course, after the machinery of this new custom house has become sufficiently clocklike in its workings, goods from the United States destined for the Klondike will be inspected, tagged, and sent in bond over the passes to the Canadian custom house to be established on Lake Bennett in just the same way as it is done with baggage belonging to passengers on Michigan Central trains going from Buffalo to Chicago. Twelve Canadian customs officials have started for the interior where they will set up an office on the portage between Lakes Bennett and Tagish, a point by which all Yukon or Klondike travelers must pass if they start from Dyea or Skagway. The rate of duty will average about $30 on the average outfit of a Yukoner. The officers are well armed, and will have the assistance of the mounted police to enforce the collection of duties. Further down the river will be stationed guards to intercept any one who might elude the vigilance of the officers.

American miners who have investigated the question, assert that the treaty between Russia and Great Britain provided that the Yukon Porcupine, and Skeena rivers should be free for commercial purposes and exempted from the imposition of custom duties. The Canadians evade the point at issue by claiming that prospectors crossing the mountain ranges to the lakes or head waters of the Yukon do not go into the territory via any of the rivers mentioned, but that they cross Canadian territory, and before they can reach the Yukon the duty is exacted.

The Canadian officers are taking with them a full year's supplies, and with the assistance of the mounted police propose to maintain an official monthly mail service, for official purposes only, between the Klondike and Ottawa.

In conclusion, here are a few pointers dictated by experience for the benefit of the Klondiker. For the most part their observance will involve but little trouble, and, on the other hand, will add vastly to one's comfort while in the frozen lands:

Do not waste a single ounce of anything, even if you do not like it. Put it away and it will come handy when you will like it.

If it is ever necessary to cache a load of provisions, put all articles next to the ground which will be most affected by heat, providing at the same time that dampness will not affect their food properties to any great extent. After piling your stuff, carefully heap heavy rocks over it. Take your compass bearings and, making a written note of nearby landmarks, indicate the direction in which they lie from your cache. If possible, align your cache exactly between north and south of two given prominent marks. In this way, even though covered by snow, you can locate your 'existence.' Do not forget that this may be the proper name for it at some future time.

Shoot a dog, if you have to, behind the base of the skull; a horse between the ears, ranging downward. Press the trigger of your rifle. Do not pull it. You should never grab the gun barrel when the temperature is 30° below zero. Be careful that snow does not plug the barrel. If it does, do not fire the gun as it will probably burst.

A little dry grass or hay in the inside of your mittens, next to your hands, will help retain the heat, especially when they get damp from the moisture of your hands. After taking off your mittens, remove the hay and dry it. Failing that, throw it away.

If by any chance you are traveling across a plain (no trail) in a fog or a blinding snowstorm, either of which will prevent you from taking your bearings, camp and do not move, no matter what anyone may urge, until the weather becomes clear again.

Keep all the drawstrings on your clothing in good repair. Always use your goggles when the sun is bright on snow. A fellow is often tempted to leave them off. This could result in snow blindness.

Travel as much on clear ice toward your goal as possible in the spring. Never pull sledges over snow, especially when it is soft or crusty.

If you build a sledge for extreme cold do not use steel runners. Make wooden ones, and freeze water on them before starting out. Repeat the process if the sled begins to drag and screech.

In building a sledge use lashing entirely. Bolts and screws rack a sledge to pieces in rough going, while lashing will "give".

Take plenty of tow for packing possible cracks in your boat, also two pounds of good putty, some canvas and, if possible, a small can of tar or white lead.

Establish camp rules, especially regarding the food. Allot rations, less while idle than when at work, and also varying with the seasons. A man requires less food, or at any rate less of certain kinds, in warm than in cold weather.

Keep your furs in good repair. One little slit may cause you untold agony during a march in a heavy storm. You never know when such a storm will overtake you.

No man can continuously drag more than his own weight.

Remember this is a fact.

Be sure during the winter to watch your footgear carefully. Change wet stockings before they freeze, or you may lose a toe or foot.

Keep the hood of your kooletah back from your head if not too cold, and allow the moisture from your body to escape that way. If your furs get wet dry them in a medium temperature. Do not hold them near a fire.

When your nose is bitterly cold, stuff both nostrils with fur, cotton, wool, or anything else soft enough. The pain will cease.

Never attempt to carry more than 40 pounds of stuff over a stiff climb, at least the first day.

In cases of extreme cold at toes and heel, wrap a piece of fur over each extremity.

Keep your sleeping bag clean. If it becomes inhabited with vermin freeze the inhabitants out.

Remember, success follows economy and persistency on an expedition like yours.

White snow over a crevasse, if hard, is safe, yeLlow or dirty color, never.

Do not eat snow or ice. Go thirsty until you can melt it.

Shoot a deer behind the left shoulder or in the head.

Choose your bunk as far from your tent door as possible.

Keep a fire hole open near your camp.

The man who knows little now will come back knowing more than he who knew it all before starting.

A Woman Pioneer in the Klondike and Alaska

Emma Kelly

The confirmation in the summer of 1897 of rich gold discoveries in the Northwest Territory, set in motion a vast army of fortune seekers bound for the Klondike District, coming from all parts of the world and from all trades, stations and walks in life. Trains reaching the Pacific Coast brought thousands of eager, restless Argonauts, who, transferring to the steamers for the north, loaded all vessels to their utmost capacity. Of the vast number who went many were properly equipped and supplied with provisions, while many others were inadequately supplied for the hardships of the rigorous climate of the gold-fields of the Northwest. At Skagway and Dyea the entrances to Chilkoot and White Passes, many of the vast throng established themselves as best they could in winter quarters, while thousands, discouraged, returned to the States with each boat on its southern trip.

Joining the great hegira, on the tenth day of September, 1897, I left Topeka, Kan., for the Klondike country, in the interest of a Chicago mining syndicate. I chose that season of the year, thinking I could go in with dogs, sledding it over the ice on the winter trail.

From Seattle, I took passage on the steamer *Willamett*, which sailed on the 23rd of September, for Dyea. The trip up the ocean at that season of the year was most delightful; the coast scenery the grandest imaginable.

Ten hours after leaving Juneau we found ourselves closely landlocked at the head of Chilkoot Inlet; about a mile and a half from Skagway – Skagway, at that time a terror to miner and mariner alike.

In a sort of wedge between the mountains, the spot which heretofore, had not known the trail of white man suddenly became a city of tents, eventually attaining a population aggregating nearly twenty thousand people and then dwindling to about five thousand. In the Skagway of the present, houses and stores have taken the place of tents, while vessels arrive daily, with passengers and merchandise for the interior. It is the starting point of the White Pass and Yukon

Railway, which is now running trains daily over this once terrible route.

One can scarcely imagine a spot more bleak and uninviting than the Skagway of tents.

The few packers who were engaged late in the season on the Skagway trail charged thirty-eight cents a pound to carry over the trail. And White Pass had been almost deserted for Chilkoot, over which the trip could be made any time during the winter, if one undertakes it with a sufficient number of men to carry his goods. There seemed at that time, no possible hope of reaching the rivers of the north by way of White Pass in winter. Two months of almost ceaseless rain had made the ground a bog-hole, the trail was knee to waist-deep, and practically impassable.

Horses, mules, oxen, dogs and goats imported in large numbers, as pack animals, proved useless, while inexperience, added to inadequacy of food supplies for the poor animals, caused hundreds of them to die on the trail, forming a long line indicative of man's folly and inhumanity in his thirst for gold.

About five hundred people were at Dyea when I reached there. Some, however, were going over the Lake pass, experiencing but little difficulty compared with the Skagway route. Previous to my arrival, the incessant rains had so honeycombed and loosened the eastern glacier as to cause it to drop into the lake, throwing vast volumes of water down the throat of the cañon, and while sacrificing the life of one poor unfortunate, this occurrence resulted beneficially to those who were to come later; the mad rush of the torrent having washed portions of the trail clean of mud and mire, leaving it greatly improved.

On the first of October, I had my outfit, consisting of a thousand pounds of goods and provisions, safely landed at Dyea, but being so late in the season and more especially on account of the terrific blizzards of the day before on the summit, I found it impossible to procure experienced packers, the natives refusing to attempt the pass after the winter blizzards had set in. All with whom I talked advised me not to go on, saying I would never be able to 'make it' that no man could and for me—a woman—it was worse than hopeless.

Being alone, not even knowing the name of any one north of

Seattle, I was obliged to rely wholly upon my own judgment.

I learned of the few returning packers from Lake Lindeman, that several parties who had been at the Lake three or four weeks had completed their boats and were ready to start across the lakes. I was told that I might be able to secure passage with some of the parties whose boats were ready, so I determined to reach Lindeman, if possible, before the boats left.

Very few attempt crossing the Pass at that season, it being too late for the summer trail, while the weather is not sufficiently settled or the snow of sufficient depth to be used as a winter trail. I secured Healy and Wilson's pack train to carry my goods as far as Sheep Camp, the foot of the Pass, twelve miles from Dyea. But how to get my thousand pounds over the Pass to the Lake, from Sheep Camp, a distance of eighteen miles, including climbing the summit, which makes it seem about eighteen thousand miles, was a problem to be solved. I thought at first to pick up a few returning packers at Sheep Camp, but then I realized they knew too well of the storm of the day before, raging on the summit, and hence would never agree to risk their lives.

In this dilemma a happy thought occurred to me. I determined to go to the steamer in the harbor and try to secure deck-hands to pack my goods over the Pass. I succeeded in inducing ten men to go with me, telling them if they would go to Sheep Camp, I would feed them for two or three days, and pay fifty cents for each pound they carried from Sheep Camp on to Lindeman. My men made a motley combination: one Dago, one Negro, a Swede, a Frenchman, an Indian half-breed and a German; the other four being simply nondescript.

With my men I set out the following morning for Sheep Camp, in the midst of a terrific blizzard, the sleet seemingly driven into our faces like needles, over one of the roughest trails of a rough country. The trail, worn deep, was made heavy and difficult of passage in its winding course through the woods and along the dry channel of the river, alternating between stones and sand, covered in places with muck and criss-crossed with roots of trees; farther on making a number of rugged ascents and descents, following close one after the other, and rising hundreds of feet above the river-bed.

It was a long, hard climb in the face of such a storm, but the most difficult part of my task was to maintain my courage, and "jollying" the packers into cheerfulness, my constant fear being that they would throw down their packs and quit me.

In passing over that weary, wearing twelve-mile stretch, we crossed one little stream sixty-one times, the waters of which are very, very swift, and of course ice-cold. In wading, the water came almost to the knees, and in some places to the waist. At those places I would get on the back of one of the packers and let him carry me over.

Pack-horses which have worked on the trail six or eight months, know thoroughly every inch of the terrible route, so with my men I fell directly in the rear of the horse pack train which carried my goods, and plodding along in the storm upon the heavy trail through the cañon, I arrived at Sheep Camp at five o'clock in the evening.

Sheep Camp was then a little town largely composed of tents, and I soon found a bunk-house and lunch counter in a rather low building—perhaps twenty-five by fifty feet—called the Palmer House, in which were gathered about fifty men returning from Lindeman. The building was dark and gloomy, possibly from its lack of windows, or from the amount of tobacco smoke in it, through which one could scarcely see.

When I entered the place and told those present I was on my way over the summit, they threw up their hands in horror, and thought it was their duty to stop me, assuring me it was suicidal for any one to attempt it at that season of the year. They warned me of the terrible storm raging, and what an awful condition the trail was in.

The tales of their trials and experiences of course made me uneasy, not because of the real danger, but because I was afraid they would put mischief into the heads of my packers, who might refuse to go on with me. I thought the best course to pursue was to keep my packers away from those men who were so full of the stories of the hardships of the trail, so I pitched my tent in the mud, snow and sleet, near the bunk-house, where I corralled my men, keeping them with difficulty away from the regular packers.

Even so, some of my men came to me and said they did not think it best for them to try going over the summit. I told them if I could go they certainly could, and for the time I succeeded in convincing them that I had more courage than any of them. By this means I kept them to their contract. I told them, however, if the weather should be too severe the next day, we would wait twenty-four hours, but every minute's delay at that time meant the probability of being shut in with the ice so much farther from Dawson.

In case I might be able to reach the lakes before the boats started across, I made an arrangement with an Indian to have a light, birch-bark canoe brought over the summit, with which I would have made the trip with an Indian as my boatman.

The trail from Sheep Camp to Lake Lindeman was strewn with packs of provisions. Packers halting, discouraged, had thrown down their loads and turned back. Hundreds of sacks of flour, bacon, beans and all the different staples which had to be carried into the country marked their route.

At the camp I received the first news of the scarcity of food in Dawson, and I knew that it would not be safe for me to move in with one ounce less than my thousand pounds, so I fully made up my mind that if I kept the packs on the backs of my men and started from Sheep Camp, I would be absolutely merciless, heartless, and severe with them until they landed all my goods at the lakes. My life was as good as theirs and I felt that it might depend on every ounce of food I took in.

The following day at Sheep Camp the storm was the most severe ever known in that locality. I delayed one day, which seemed like a year to me, entertaining and "jollying" the motley crowd of packers, to keep them away from men of experience.

The third day there was only a trifle of wind, and the sun was warm and bright. I was up at five o'clock in the morning, got breakfast for the packers, after which each of them took a hundred pounds on his back, and by seven o'clock we bade farewell to Sheep Camp.

At ten o'clock, Stone House, just at the foot of the steep climb, was reached. The sun was warm, and we had not suffered at all from the cold.

From Stone House, or the Scales, as it is called, the ascent is precipitous and rugged, rising two and a half miles at an angle of forty-five degrees, to the mist-clad summit. Immense boulders perhaps forty or fifty feet in length and covered with snow, skirted or crossed the trail, which farther on traverses a vast glacier and winds its way along precipices hundreds of feet in depth. The foot of the pass marks the line of vegetation and beyond this, the unfortunate pedestrian, slipping, has no other hold than the rocks upon which he may have fallen.

I placed my packers in a line ahead of me and started for the top. We could only proceed a few steps, when we were compelled to stop and rest in order to get our breath. Thus we proceeded by slow stages to the summit. The trail, covered with snow and ice, made it dangerous and wearisome.

When about a mile from the summit we met a man returning from the lakes. The foremost packer called to him and inquired how far it was to the summit. The man looked at him and answered the question with:

"How many pounds have you on your back?"

"One hundred."

"Then it is just one hundred thousand miles to you," said the stranger.

I really believe it would seem that to those who were carrying packs.

When I myself asked the man the distance, he noticed that I was without a pack, and smiling, said:

"About a mile and a half."

In fact, the Dago expressed it pretty well. When some one said to him, "Pretty steep, partner," he answered, "It's more than steep; it leans back."

At one o'clock we all sat down to rest on the highest rock of the summit and, be assured, it was a relief to me to look back over the trail to Sheep Camp and realize I was over the severest part of my trip, safely, and with all my goods.

There was about five feet of snow on the summit and, as we went down the mountains to Lindeman, I thought of the remaining eleven miles to the lake with joy, without a fear then of my packers abandoning me.

At half past nine my packers laid down their loads on the banks of Lake Lindeman. How tired we were!

We had made eighteen miles from seven o'clock in the morning to half past nine that night, over one of the most terrible mountain passes in the world.

We camped at the lake, and fared quite well on bacon and beans.

But I was too anxious to think much of eating, and as there were a number of tents lighted up, I went among them making inquiries for parties who had completed their boats, to get passage with one of them. The second tent I entered I think the men felt rather sorry for me, because if a girl ever looked worn out and tired I did that night.

The man told me that a party of twenty-two men, most of them from Nevada and California, who had packed over the summit together, and had built their boats of timber they had cut and whip-sawed into lumber, were about ready for the voyage.

Their little craft were about the size of an ordinary row-boat. Seven men were to ride in each of two of them, and eight in another; and each man carried seven or eight hundred pounds of "grub". The men were dubious of being able to accommodate me, with my heavy outfit and "Klondike", a fine Newfoundland shepherd dog I had brought with me from Seattle, but as they were all dead broke, and the Canadian custom duties had to be paid at Tagish Lake, my offer of one hundred and twenty-five dollars for passage was accepted.

The next morning, about ten o'clock, I was notified that the party would start at noon. I was lying on the ground, rolled up in a blanket, and so sore and stiff from my long climb in the water, slush, mud, ice and snow of the day before, that I could not get up without assistance. But I did not dare say anything about it lest I would be thought a nuisance, and so had to grin and bear it, and hobble around the best I could all morning.

By one o'clock the boats were loaded and we pushed off.

Lindeman is connected by a short stream with Lake Bennett, on the shore of which I came upon a grave with a rough wooden cross, inscribed:

"J. Matthews, Age 26."

I learned that, after losing his outfit on the summit, this young man went back to Dyea, and invested his last dollar in a second "grub stake," but again lost his loaded boat in this treacherous channel. His resources exhausted, he gave up in despair, and shot himself.

Gathering a few green spruce boughs I placed them in the snow over his grave. My thought was for a lone woman grieving for the absence of one who could never return.

The Skagway trail over the mountain reaches Lake Bennett, and the evening we were there a most heartless man, who had a pack-train of horses, arrived over the trail, the horses all carrying heavy packs. The animals had not had any food for days, as there was nothing upon which they could graze, and even had there been, their owner was so cruel and avaricious for every dollar to be had, that it is doubtful if he would have allowed them time to feed.

They were simply racks of bones, scarcely any flesh upon their ribs or bodies, having made several trips over the Skagway trail during the summer.

About half a mile from the place where they were to be unloaded, the five in the lead of the train gave out, completely, and one which had fallen down was severely beaten with a rough stick in the hands of the cruel owner. The poor brute staggered to its feet only to take a few steps, when it fell a second time. The other four, as they stood trembling and swaying from weakness and hunger, seemed ready to drop dead.

I watched the man as long as I could stand it, then ran over to my war-sack, got my revolver, and while he was at the rear of the pack-train, shot the animal in the head. I knew it was only a matter of a few hours before the poor beast would succumb, and I thought death would put it out of its misery.

On coming up, the enraged owner started for me, using some very profane language. He was even about to strike me, but I had twenty-two men to defend me and make him swallow every word he said. The only thing I was censured for by my companions was that I did not shoot the man.

Had the bodies of the dead horses on the Skagway trail at that time, been laid together, they would have covered a distance of more than fifteen miles. All of them had originally been fine animals, but through want of food and proper treatment, their bones marked the fearful route of the deadly trail.

At Lake Bennett we remained in camp for two days.

The wind was blowing a gale, with sleet falling, when we started out on the thirty miles across Lake Bennett, at ten o'clock in the morning.

My first experience of sleeping out, without a tent, was on Division Island, half way across the lake, where we camped for the night. Surrounded by water, and with the sky as my only covering,

I rolled myself in blankets before the camp fire.

We had our breakfast, and as we pushed away from the island, saw on the opposite shore, on the mainland, a solitary man who called to us. We rowed over and found he was one of the three men with whom we had started from the head of the lake the day before, and just as we were landing on the island for the night, he and his companions, were trying to make a landing on the mainland, when the treacherous waters of the lake capsized the boat. His companions had both drowned and the entire outfit had been lost, the one man barely reaching the shore.

We took him in the boat with us as far as the custom house.

On Tagish Lake we found the custom house officials erecting their cabins for winter quarters. There were a good many boats tied up there, unable to pay custom duties, the amount of which the owners were working out in helping erect the government buildings.

The custom house officers warned us to push on as rapidly as possible, and to travel by day and by night, if we expected to get through to Dawson, as we were in danger of being closed in by the ice. As the mornings and evenings were very foggy, we were unable to make more than twenty or twenty-five miles a day.

Sluggish in the wider parts, the stream narrows between the mountains where the water is forced through at great velocity. Miles Cañon is the most famous of these narrows, and approaching it, swinging round in the river, we nearly collided with a boat, lying on its side against the rocks, with a hole in the centre-board. It told a gruesome tale of wreck and disaster; I soon recovered my nerve, however, and announced that I would ride through the cañon in a boat, but the men vehemently protested against it. But, somehow, I could not make up my mind that it was such a dangerous thing to attempt, and my womanly nature seemed to tell me that I could go through and all would be well.

I wanted to make the trip. I wanted to see and feel what manner of thing this so-called danger is, which men court so freely, but which women may only read and hear of.

I was informed that no man who had ever guided a boat through Miles Cañon had yet consented to take a woman through its seething, foaming waters. But I insisted on going through, and go through I did.

How did it feel? Well, to me it was a delightful experience.

The stream is very swift for a long distance, before the entrance to the cañon is reached, and as the prow of the boat turned into the stream and was caught by the current, I felt as if I were being swung around by some mighty, powerful engine, and then shot forward at a terrific rate. I felt as if the boat would certainly glide out from under me. Faster and faster we went, until it seemed as if we had been speeding along for at least two or three minutes, while as a fact, the distance made required only thirty seconds.

When we slowed up a little, we felt the waters swell beneath us, churning the boat on all sides. At that point, the cañon widens a little, the waters, thrown out of the main channel, are dashed, foaming and seething, against the projecting sides of the granite walls, which hold them in their narrow course. Then, if you succeed in keeping in the narrow channel, you glide into a very narrow part of the rapids, and in a second more you shoot down and out of the mouth of the cañon, into the turbulent waters below. After hard pulling, a landing is effected and the thing is done, excepting for a mad desire to repeat it.

If you would know the sensation of a ride through that cañon go you to the "chutes," shoot them, but imagine you are going twice as fast. Imagine, also, that on each side of you a perpendicular wall of rock, with sharp, angular projections, rises to a height of three hundred feet, and that under and around you are about forty sawmills running at full speed. Then you may have a faint conception of a boat ride through Miles Cañon.

Through this cañon, the distance is a fraction less than a mile, and the time occupied in making the passage in a boat is one and a half minutes.

Between the cañon and the White Horse Rapids, it is only two or three miles. Before reaching the rapids, we landed and walked round for a preliminary look which decided the men to go through with boats loaded. At this point, nearly every one makes a portage around, the distance about a mile and a quarter, running their boats through empty.

When I said I would go through the rapids with them, we had a rehash of all the argument, pro and con, that we had at the cañon.

They all said, as one man, "I won't," but you know just what show a man's "I won't" has, against a woman's "I will." Well, there, as at the cañon, I had my way, and I enjoyed the experience of a ride through that great bug-a-boo of the trip to Dawson.

Are the White Horse Rapids dangerous and fear-inspiring? Well, perhaps they are, but if so, I can only say that I claim no credit for having done anything which seemed very dangerous, to me. I gained my point and came through them on the sixteenth day of October, 1897.

They seemed to be much more dangerous than those at the cañon, it is true. The foaming, angry waters, piled high in the channel, looked as if some immense stern-wheel boat was running, bottom up, beneath them, churning and lashing them into fury. As for the ride through, I do not know when I enjoyed anything so much in my life. I snugly stowed myself away in the prow of the boat, the men got ready, the word was given, the line cast loose, and we were off. The boat gave a screech, a groan, seemed to stretch itself and reach its nose out to every bounding billow, which helped to carry it forward rapidly, to the foaming riffles near the end of the rapids.

On we went, faster and faster yet. The man at the sweep never took his eye from the course, never once missed a puff at this pipe, excepting now and then to sing out to first one and then another of the oarsmen to "Give her h—l," so as to keep the boat's prow straight on.

A few seconds and we struck the riffles. The wild waves rocked and rolled our boat, and occasionally broke over us. The spray rose so thick and high we could not see the shores; the very air seeming a sea of misty spray. It was simply glorious! All too soon we rode into comparatively smooth, yet rapid water. A few more strokes of the oars sent us in to shore, and the ride was over, leaving a sensation never to be forgotten.

I went back to go through in the second boat, but the man who was steering told me there would be room for but three who were working at the oars. I said, "Let me take an oar." I so thoroughly enjoyed the sensation of the ride through the rapids, I wanted to repeat it as often as possible.

On the seat by my side sat a minister, who was also going to take an oar. The man at the helm sang out, "Give her h—l," upon which the minister gave a groan and a hard pull. When we were safely through he said:

"Miss Kelly, did you note the language which the man steering the boat used?"

I said I had noticed it, and with a look of relief he responded:

"Well, you noticed I gave her h—l, didn't you?"

As I have said, I did not feel that I did a very dangerous thing, and at no time felt the least fear. I must confess, though, that the hearty congratulations and cheers of so many big, strong men, for "the first woman who ever took an oar in a boat going through White Horse," gave me a momentary feeling of elation that I had really accomplished a most dangerous feat.

Lake Leberge is the last of the beautiful chain of lakes between the pass and Lewis River, the head waters of the Yukon.

Each day, as we proceeded farther north, and it became later in the season, the days shorter, the drift ice thicker, and the temperature lower, it was, oh so much colder! This checked our speed, and we were able to make only from ten to eighteen miles a day. Finally, we could only drift with the ice; it forming in large cakes, eight by ten to eighteen by twenty feet in size. The blocks would wedge around our boats so tightly and closely, it was impossible to use the oars. Two of the men stationed themselves on either end of the boat to push away the largest and most dangerous pieces. When we got into the current, we drifted along with the ice at pretty fair speed and felt comparatively easy. But the water was at a very low stage, and we were liable to swing on to a sand-bar, to be blocked out in the middle of the Yukon for the winter.

The ice formed a barricade on the sides of our boat, by freezing a foot in thickness on all sides, thus protecting us from the larger cakes which might otherwise have jammed into us and done irreparable injury.

The ice cakes, ground together by the current turning them, formed in perfect circles.

Sitting all day long in the little craft, cramped for want of room, with rain, sleet and snow falling continually and avoiding losing time by making no stop for warm noon lunch, eating the frozen bread, bacon and beans left over from breakfast, the thermometer at eighteen to twenty degrees below zero; as evening approached working our boat from the middle of the Yukon through the drift ice to reach the shore at dark; making camp on three feet of snow, sitting on the snow to eat a warm supper, then rolling up in wet and frozen blankets stretched out on the snow, with occasional cuttings of spruce boughs for bedding—this was my experience of camp life.

Fort Selkirk is an old Indian trading post, there being also a mission and many cabins. All the men of the party were in favor of going into camp in warm and comfortable quarters, and sledding their outfits in, in the middle of the winter, when there would be a good trail.

We were then two hundred miles from Dawson, and I was not particularly fascinated with the idea of walking that distance in the snow, helping break trail on snow shoes, and risking my outfit being hauled in, so I insisted on the men going on. I urged them to try it another day, thinking it would be better to make a few miles at a time, drifting in a boat, than drawing a sled over an unbroken trail.

During the last ten days before Dawson was reached, we could only make five, six or seven miles a day, the ice blocking so thickly, the river was likely to close any minute.

One night, just after leaving Pelly we saw moose tracks in the snow. The moose is very much like the buffalo of the plains, and the flesh very rich, juicy and sweet. One of the men, who was a good shot, tracked it up the mountain about a quarter of a mile, and killed it. So we had plenty of fresh meat on our trip into Dawson.

Every day we saw from five to twenty black bear along the banks of the river. We killed two, the men keeping the skins for robes, we eating the meat, which was a little coarse, but very good. We also saw many red foxes, wolverines, and squirrels.

On the first day of November, the river was nearly blocked with ice, which was barely moving, but we worked our boats through the drifts, out into the current, and floated into Dawson, entering the great Klondike district, the richest placer camp ever discovered.

Just at dark we made a landing on the banks of the Yukon, directly in front of the little town of Dawson. We pitched our tents in the snow, where we camped for the night; our first shelter, even of a tent, for thirty days.

We were all so thoroughly pleased, and so happy that good fortune had enabled us to arrive safely in Dawson. I went to my war-sack, got out my guitar, which I had carried all the way over the summit; and, sitting on the snow around that little tent, those rugged, great-hearted men it had been my good fortune to meet and travel with, all joined with me in sincere thanksgiving—and the dear old songs of the heart and home.

Skagway and Dyea

The towns of Skagway and Dyea sprang almost instantly from the tidal flats of the Lynn Canal. Skagway was the start of the White Pass Trail and Dyea of the Chilkoot Trail. These routes had been well-traveled for centuries by Chilkat Indians and climbed past sheer mountains and glaciers. The White Pass and Chilkoot Trails were the most popular routes to the Klondike. For many stampeders this was their first glimpse of the ordeal ahead of them. Some booked passage home, choosing to cut their losses.

In the first couple of years of the gold rush, the city of Skagway was the type of frontier town we see in western movies. It had makeshift buildings with false fronts, gambling halls, saloons, dance halls and bandits. The most notorious outlaw was Jefferson "Soapy" Smith. His gang of bandits were experienced con men and thieves, many of whom were veterans from other gold rushes. Skagway was an outlaw's haven and Soapy's gang conned, cheated and stole from stampeders at will. Eventually a vigilante group formed to put an end to Soapy's empire. A gunfight followed, leaving Soapy dead, and a short time later his assailant Frank Reid also died.

Dyea was less developed and arguably less lawless, than its sister town Skagway. The first stampeders who arrived at Dyea Harbor found endless tidal flats stretching before them. Ships sat at a safe distance from shore as smaller dories and barges ferried supplies. Those who couldn't afford the excessive cost of having horses or oxen carry their poke above the high water mark faced a dilemma. As the tides advanced, these stampeders had to race madly to get their 1,500 pounds of provisions off the flats.

Little remains of Dyea today, as it only existed for a single year and was deserted when the White Pass and Yukon Route Railway was completed in 1899. It is still possible, however, to see upright posts in the sand where a pier jutted across the flats to the shallow harbor.

The Saloon In Skagway

Tappan Adney

August 21

Today a proposition is made by a man by the name of Charles Leadbetter, of San Francisco, who is just over from Dyea, to take all our stuff, not exceeding three thousand pounds when delivered to him at Dyea; to team it thence to the head of canoe navigation; there put it on his pack-train, which will carry it to The Scales, which is at the foot of the summit; there two men will be given us to help us pack our stuff over the summit—a distance of from three-quarters of a mile to a mile to Crater Lake ; there we will have to ferry it over the lake, when it will be taken on a burro train to Long Lake, where there is another ferry, and then again on the burros to Lake Lindeman, which is the point of departure. We shall be expected to help with the pack-train, if necessary, and all this he will do in return for our eight horses. It seems a reasonable proposition, except that we are surprised at the time allowed—namely, four or five days —for making the trip through to Lake Lindeman. It is agreeable news that goods are moving right along on the Dyea trail. We still have no doubt of getting through White Pass, but we gladly hail any proposition which will land us quickly and without great trouble at the head of navigation of the Yukon.

The terms do not include our boat lumber. We are advised to cut it into lengths of seven feet, suitable for horse-packing, but it has come thus far in whole lengths, and we desire to keep it so as long as possible. Accordingly, we deliver our horses, with a ton of feed, to the packer, who takes them over on a scow in tow of a tugboat, which makes trips between Dyea and Skagway as often and at such times as the tide permits. The cost for transportation is $10 a head. Our intention is to follow at the earliest date.

There is no shady side to life at Skagway; everything goes on in broad daylight or candlelight. After supper every tent is lighted up, and the streets are crowded with muddy men in from the trail. The "Pack Train" is filled with people, among whom I recognize several of my friends, who are drawn hither, like myself, by the spectacle. The tent of the biggest saloon in town is thirty by fifty feet. Entering through a single door in front, on the right hand is a rough board bar some ten or twelve feet long, with some shelves against the rear wall, on which are a few glasses and bottles. The bartender, who is evidently new to his business, apologizes for the whiskey, which is very poor and two-thirds water, and sells for 25 cents. Cigars of a two-for-five or five-cent sort, that strain one's suction powers to the limit, are sold for from 15 to 25 cents each. They keep beer also, on tap. After the lecture we received on the steamer from the United States customs officer, we are at a loss to understand how whiskey can be sold openly under the very eyes of the officers. But that is a story by itself. Along each side of the tent are the three-card Monte, the rouge-et-noir, and other layouts, but not a faro layout in the place nor in the town. The gamblers are doing big business.

A big, strapping fellow, in a yellow Mackinaw jacket, trying his luck at craps, is pointed out as having just come in over the trail from Klondike. Whether he has any dust with him I do not learn, but he is in fine health and spirits. Every man whom I have yet seen from Klondike has a splendid complexion and seems strong and robust. This fellow has a voice like a lion's, deep and resonant. Surely the Yukon cannot be so terrible if it does this to men, or else its tale of death is that of the weak and sickly.

Across the street the sound of a piano and the moving figures of men and women seen through the windows remind one that there is a dance tonight, as on every night. This piano is the only one in town, and its arrival is said to have been an event. The four women in the place are not even of the painted sort; paint might have covered up some of the marks of dissipation. Clumsy boots beat time on a dirty floor, but not with much enthusiasm. There is not sport enough to get up as much as a quadrille. The dance-house of a mining-town! Such a thing as shame is not even thought of.

Among the many who are gazing upon the unaccustomed scene, with the same absorbed interest as the youngest of us, are men whom I take to be old-timers. I asked one of these what he thought of it all.

Said he: "I was in the Salmon River mining excitement in Idaho, but I have never seen anything like this. Ten thousand people went in that winter, over a single trail across the mountains; but it was nothing like this. There has never been anything on this coast like it."

Another, who is now the mayor of a town on the Pacific coast not far from the Strait of Fuca, said, in answer to the same question: "I saw the beginning of Leadville, but it was nothing like this; there has been nothing like this."

Still another, a mining engineer from California, said: "I have never seen people act as they do here. They have lost their heads and their senses. I have never seen men behave as they do here. They have no more idea of what they are going to than that horse has. There was one fellow in the tent alongside of mine — I saw him greasing his rubber boots. I said to him, 'What are you doing that for?' 'Why, isn't that all right?' he asked. Another man came along and asked a fellow where his mining-pan was. The fellow said, 'I haven't seen any mining-pan.' Just then the man saw the pan lying along side the tent, and said, 'Here it is! Is that a mining pan? I didn't know that was a mining-pan.'"

I have talked with many others, some who had been in the Coeur d'Alene excitement on Salmon River, Idaho, and have been miners since '53 and '54. Some, whose fathers were of the old '49's, say the same thing — that the country has gone mad over this Klondike business. And all agree as to the reason — nowadays the news is carried by the telegraph and newspaper to all parts of the world, whereas formerly the excitement was all local, and had died away before word of it reached the rest of the world.

No one pretends to follow the changes that are going on here. Those who have been here a week are old-timers. When the next boat arrives people will ask questions of us in turn.

August 22

The work of unloading the vessel continues. Most of the hay and the lumber has been loaded upon a scow and hauled inshore, so that the vessel can clear for the south on time. As the quickest way to get the lumber off, six or seven of us take hold of the scow, throw the lumber into the water, and raft it ashore. It is noon before we discover that it is Sunday. Sunday makes no difference in Skagway. All the goods are now landed, and each man is carrying away what belongs to him — also some that doesn't belong to him, if there are any grounds for the vigorous complaints made to the checkers. After the confusion aboard in the hold, the wonder is that any one gets what belongs to him.

It is raining again tonight. None of the weather signs we are accustomed to in the East hold good here. A man who lived six years back of the Chilkoot Mountains says that in this part of Alaska, at this time of the year, it will be clear and cold for four days, and then it will rain four days. It has rained the four days all right, and we are looking for the four sunny ones. This wet weather is discouraging. Every one feels miserable.

August 23

Day breaks clear. It is full daylight at five or six. The sky is cloudless and the air is warm. Every one is happy.

I engage a man, who hails from Texas, with a thirty-foot dory (which he says came up in pieces from San Francisco to go over the mountain, and which he purchased for a few dollars at the beach), to take all my stuff to Dyea. The wind is piping up Lynn Canal, tossing up the whitecaps, and heavy breakers are rolling in on the beach. Our skipper is sure of his boat, so we take my own twelve hundred pounds, with the boat lumber, a ton of hay and oats, and a thousand pounds of baggage belonging to one of my fellow-passengers on the Islander who has seen both trails, and pronounces unhesitatingly in favor of Dyea. He is Monsieur l'Abbé, a lumberman and merchant from Port Arthur, Lake Superior.

Lynn Canal is a long, deep trench between towering mountains, like a great fresh-water lake. The water is only slightly salt to the taste. It is hard to believe that it is the sea. It is as cold as the melting ice from scores of glaciers on the mountaintops can make it, and a man could not swim twenty yards in such a chill. It is a marvel that any of the horses thrown overboard reached shore.

After a dangerous passage through the heavy seas that nearly swamp us with our top-heavy load, we round the point of rocks, and, with the wind behind us, are driven rapidly towards the mouth of the Dyea pass. We follow the right-hand shore, where the rocks boldly rise perpendicularly from the water, and presently meet a swift current in the mouth of the Dyea River, a stream twice the size of the Skagway, flowing seaward through a broad alluvial plain.

We go a little way, wading and dragging the boat against the current, and land in the midst of a number of tents and piles of baggage. Leadbetter himself is not here, but his teamster and wagon are, so, leaving word with Monsieur l'Abbé and another that my stuff has arrived, I go back to Skagway. After a desperate tussle against the wind, making almost no headway, we go ashore in a cove, and reach Skagway afoot.

During a temporary absence of Jim and the boy a runaway steer kicked some sparks from a fire against the back of the tent, which had burned out half the end of the tent before neighbors extinguished it. This is the story, but I think the wind blew the sparks from said neighbors' campfire. The fire, however, burned the cover and part of the leather off my camera, yet without hurting the camera. It destroyed the tripod cover without touching the tripod; it burned the gun-case without hurting the rifle; it burned some twenty pages of my diary, but took the back, where there was no writing, instead of the front leaves. The actual loss was a few envelopes. Altogether a remarkable escape.

Jim and Burghardt are ready to go to Dyea; so, giving them directions, I take my 5 x 7 camera and start in on the Skagway trail. With the perversity of Alaska weather, it begins to rain by the time the "Foot of the Hill" is reached. There are only a few horses moving in at this time of day. At the summit of the Hill the narrow trail follows the steep bank of a ravine, and here we see the first victim of the trail — a horse lying at the foot of the bank, twenty feet down, beside a small stream. It is dead now, but before it died some stakes were driven around it to keep it out of the water.

Just now we met a man who says that a horse has just tumbled off the trail and down in a hole between two or three immense boulders, and that only its head is sticking out, and that it is alive. We keep on along comparatively level boulder-strewn ground, and evidently pass the spot indicated, which is not surprising, as bushes and trees cover every spot and hide the treacherous holes. We are going on firm bottom, with numerous corduroys over muck-holes, but ankle-deep in sloppy, slimy, chocolate-colored mud. It looks perhaps worse than it is. Horses and men, bags and pack-covers, are dyed with this brown stain. Again the trail mounts the slope of the mountain, by a way so rocky that it would seem as if no horse could get up it. The smooth, flat sides of rocks slope inward, affording no foothold to a horse. We meet a young man on horseback coming down the worst of these places. We step aside and curse under our breath the man who would ride a horse down such a place. We did not know then that he had a broken foot. A corduroy bridge, sloping at an angle of fully forty degrees, was soon afterwards put over the whole length of this pitch. The logs give a hold to the shoe-calks that the rocks do not. Where the horses slide and scrape the rocks it looks like the work of chisels.

The trail climbs from terrace to terrace, or follows the brink of perpendicular cliffs, but all is so covered with luxurious vegetation that the heights above and the depths below do not impress one. We come to an empty packsaddle, and know something has happened here, as down the mountainside the bushes are bruised, as if some heavy body had rolled down. We need no one to tell us that over the cliff a horse has rolled hundreds of feet, and lies out of sight among the bushes. Again an almost unbearable stench announces an earlier victim.

Every man we meet tells of the trials of the trail. Anxious and weary are they. I saw one halfway up a hill asleep on his pack, with his closed eyes towards the sky and the rain pattering on his face, which was as pale as death. It gave me a start, until I noticed his deep breathing. A little way on three horses lie dead, two of them half buried in the black quagmire, and the horses step over their bodies, without a look, and painfully struggle on. Now (only two miles by survey, but three or four to every one who passes over) the trail begins its steep plunge down the side of Porcupine Ridge, switching back and forth. At the turns it seems as if nothing could prevent a loaded horse from going clean over. The bank goes downward nearly perpendicular several hundred feet, when one lands in the narrow gorge of the Porcupine, a branch of the Skagway. Here are more tents — another breathing-spot. The Porcupine is crossed by a corduroy bridge, and the ascent begins again. The surface of the rocks is now more in evidence, and the trail leads over these, slippery with trampled mud.

Gradually, stage-by-stage, the trail rises, following the sloping shelves of bare rock, so smooth as to afford no foothold. In one place, for two or three hundred feet, the shelf that the trail follows slopes upward, and at the same time outward. A horse here needs something more than calked shoes to hold on by. No safe trail can be made until steps are cut bodily into these places. Where there are no rocks there are boggy holes. It is all rocks and mud — rocks and mud.

Suddenly the trail opens out on the mountainside, and a magnificent view is presented to the eye. Across the valley a rugged mountain, sloping, a mile in height; and down far away to the westward the blue hills and the smoke of Skagway, with Lynn Canal showing a three-cornered patch of lighter color. It is magnificent.

Five or six hundred feet below we can hear the roar of the waters. Another pitch downward and we are again on the Skagway River. Why the trail did not follow the Skagway, without climbing these two terrible ridges, none of us can comprehend. The railway, of course, will follow the riverbed, or else tunnel through the Chilkoot Mountains. Tents and piles of goods are scattered thickly along the trail. No one knows how many people there are. We guess five thousand — there may be more — and two thousand head of horses. Of course there are means of knowing, if one has kept track of arrivals of steamers at Skagway, but no one I know has bothered. A steamer arrives and empties several hundred people and tons of goods into the mouth of the trail, and the trail absorbs them as a sponge drinks up water. They are lost amid the gulches and trees.

Every one is discouraged. Dirty and muddy from head to foot, wet and tired, it is no wonder. Men who have been on the trail two weeks are no farther than this. They tell of parties who have reached even the summit, and there, disheartened, have sold out and come back. Some say boats have been carried as far as the summit and there deserted. Others say boats cannot be taken over at all. The trail is lined from Skagway to the "Foot of the Hill" with boat lumber enough, as one person said, to make a corduroy road the length of the trail.

Darkness comes on, and I stop for the night with two old prospectors, alongside a granite boulder as big as a house. Against its flat side, and partially protected by it, they have piled their stuff, in the very spot I should have chosen for my bed. They have a small fire going, and their three horses are tied to bushes near by, munching their oats. The men are well provided with blankets, which, when supper is over, are spread out on the ground beside the pile of goods, while a rope is stretched to keep the horses from tramping on the bed. They are both old miners. One, a man of fifty-four, had been in former mining excitements, and he had seen bad trails. Now every sort of opinion has been expressed of this trail; and when a man tells me a trail is bad, that counts for nothing until I know what his idea of bad is. I asked this man what he thought of this trail. Said he:

"I have seen worse trails for a short distance — five or six miles or so — but this is the worst I have ever seen for the distance. I went in over the trail when it was first cut through, and I called it then a good trail, but I predict that if the rains keep up it will be impossible to get a horse over."

It has stopped raining. We lay our coats under our heads for pillows, and our guns under the coats, and turn in. Of course we cannot take off anything but our coats and boots. We wake up in the middle of the night with the rain in our faces. I put my broad hat over my face, turn over, and go to sleep again.

August 24

We are up at five o'clock. Half an hour later I am on the trail. There are several others on the trail with their packs. Everybody, no matter how dirty or tired, would give any price for a photograph of himself, "just to send back home to show what I am like." The men imagine their friends would be surprised to see them begrimed and unshaven and muddy under their packs.

We cross the Skagway on another corduroy bridge, where a fine view up and down the valley is to be had. Near here a stream of water comes down the mountainside out of the clouds, and before it is halfway down it divides into several more streams, which find their way into the Skagway in a dozen places. The dullest or least sentimental man on the trail cannot but stop to admire this beautiful sight. From this bridge the trail follows the valley of the Skagway, the ground being flat and boggy.

The main summit is still six or seven (estimated) miles distant, and, as it is raining, I put in at the tent of three hardy fellows whom I saw the first day at Skagway, after feed for their two horses. They have been two weeks on the trail. They tell me one of their horses is played out this side of Porcupine.

"He fell over a bank forty or fifty feet, and was on the trail next day all right, but he must have been hurt inside. He's all shot to hell now."

Two of them go back to where they left the horse, and return before night. They have a little fun at first by saying they sold the horse for $125 to a man that came along and wanted to buy.

"Of course we told him we couldn't recommend the horse, but it was a horse!"

This does not seem unreasonable to us, as any kind of a horse brings whatever one asks for it. At length one of them says: "No; but we did offer it to a man for $10. He said he didn't want it. Then we offered to give it to him. He said he didn't want it even at that price. Then we asked him for a gun to shoot it with, and he lent us a revolver and we shot it."

I saw one of these men afterwards. He told me they had sold their other horse, as they found it was cheaper to pack their goods on their own backs than to carry horse-feed eight or nine miles from Skagway. A few horses are passing along in the rain. One or two large oxen go by loaded with three hundred and more pounds. It is astonishing what they will carry. And then, when they are there, they can be killed and eaten. Doubtless a horse can be eaten also, but most people have preferences.

Every one is downhearted. So near the summit, yet so great has been their struggle that hardly one expects to get over at all, but is seriously discussing the best place to winter. Said one "I mean to go in if it takes all winter. If a man can hunt and get a caribou, he need not mind it."

None of them feel like going back, but most of them regret having started. All of them blame the misrepresentation about the trail, and there are many anxious inquiries about how it is at Dyea.

The trail along the bed of the river is a continuous mire, knee-deep to men and horses. Here and there is a spot where a spring branch crosses the trail, and in such spots, which are twenty to thirty feet across, there is simply no bottom. One such hole is beside our camp. Of the first train of five horses and three men that I saw go by, three horses and two men got in, and with difficulty got out. After that every horse went in to his tail in the mud, but, after desperate struggles, got upon solid ground. There are worse holes than this. The trail crosses the river by two more bridges, and then continues on to the summit by a road equally bad but no worse than what we have come over. Past the summit no one at present knows anything of the trail, only that a few persons have got through to the Lakes, including two or three women. The trail is all but impassable, yet some are plugging along. These men, it is predicted, will lose their horses in three or four days. Some say that something must be done; they are willing to put in work, but are not willing unless others help.

There is no common interest. The selfish are crowding on, every man for himself. Unless something is done soon the trail will be blocked, and then no one will get through.

"It's no use going around these mud-holes," says one of my fellows. "The swamp is all alike. The only thing to do is to make corduroy bridges every foot of the way before there will be a trail. I am willing to start to-morrow and bridge the holes above here."

No wonder they are discouraged. Rain, rain, all the time — no sunshine up in these mountains; tent pitched in a mud-hole, bed made on the stumps of bushes, blankets and everything else wet and muddy. They are trying to dry out a hair-seal cap and some socks before a miserable fire. Even the wood is wet, and will only smoke and smolder.

August 25

I remain all night in their tent, and early this morning set out to come back, having seen enough of the trail to know what the rest is like. I should like to go on past the summit; but my goods are at Dyea — indeed, as things go in this country, I cannot be sure that I have any goods left at all.

I have made careful inquiry about the loss of horses on the trail. The number at the present time is probably about twenty actually killed, with considerably more badly hurt or temporarily laid up. Each day now about four horses are killed. The number is bound to increase as the trail grows worse (which is nearly impossible) and the horses grow weak under the strain and from lack of care. When the sun and rains of summer shall have melted the snow of the Chilkoots, the White Pass trail will be paved with the bones of horses, and the ravens and foxes will have feasted as never before until the white man sought a new way across the great mountain. As many horses as have come in alive, just so many will bleach their bones by the pine-trees and in the gulches—for none will go out.

A little while ago contracts were taken by the packers at 20 cents, then 25 cents, a pound. Just now $650 was paid for a thousand pounds, while $1000 for a thousand pounds was offered and refused.

Yesterday a horse deliberately walked over the face of Porcupine Hill. Said one of the men who saw it:

"It looked to me, sir, like suicide. I believe a horse will commit suicide, and this is enough to make them; they don't mind the hills like they do these mud-holes." He added, "I don't know but that I's rather commit suicide, too, than be driven by some of the men on this trail."

The Chilkoot and Dead Horse Trails

The barbarity and cruelty of the White Pass Trail is difficult to imagine. This trail led from Skagway through the dense coastal rain forest to a relatively low summit and the headwaters of the Yukon River. The White Pass Trail was about 600 feet lower than the popular Chilkoot Trail to the north but was far more rugged.

The White Pass Trail was a narrow path that followed the Skagway River for much of its course. This path was steep and had numerous sink holes where horses easily broke ankles and were impaled by stumps. Gold fever drove stampeders to abuse their half-starved horses in the most horrible manner. When the horses dropped from exhaustion or broken limbs, the line of miners and pack animals walked over them until they became part of the trail. For this reason the White Pass became known as the trail of "Dead Horses." More than 3,000 horses died during the first year of the gold rush.

The Chilkoot Trail was swarmed by thousands of stampeders. This ancient Indian trade route to the interior became famous worldwide. The wealthy stampeders hired Indian packers to ferry enormous mounds of supplies across this rugged landscape. Others simply pulled cases and packs onto their backs and like ants, struggled along the trail. Many speculate that more stampeders would have perished without the sage advice and help of the Indian packers and guides. The Chilkoot was the preferred overland route to the Yukon although it posed many challenges to all who traveled on this trail.

By 1899 a railway was completed through the White Pass Valley to the city of Whitehorse and these trails were largely forgotten.

The Spell of the Yukon
Robert Service

I wanted the gold, and I sought it;
  I scrabbled and mucked like a slave.
Was it famine or scurvy, I fought it;
  I hurled my youth into a grave.
I wanted the gold, and I got it —
  Came out with a fortune last fall, —
Yet somehow life's not what I thought it,
  And somehow the gold isn't all.

No! There's the land. (Have you seen it?)
  It's the cussedest land that I know,
From the big, dizzy mountains that screen it
  To the deep, deathlike valleys below.
Some say God was tired when He made it;
  Some say it's a fine land to shun;
Maybe; but there's some as would trade it
  For no land on earth — and I'm one.
You come to get rich (damned good reason);
  You feel like an exile at first.
You hate it like hell for a season,
  And then you are worse than the worst.
It grips you like some kinds of sinning;
  It twists you from foe to a friend;
It seems it's been since the beginning;
  It seems it will be to the end.

I've stood in some mighty-mouthed hollow
  That's plumb-full of hush to the brim.
I've watched the big, husky sun wallow
  In crimson and gold, and grow dim,
Till the moon set the pearly peaks gleaming,

And the stars tumbled out, neck and crop;
And I've thought that I surely was dreaming,
  With the peace o' the world piled on top.

The summer — no sweeter was ever;
  The sunshiny woods all athrill;
The grayling aleap in the river,
  The bighorn asleep on the hill.
The strong life that never knows harness;
  The wilds where the caribou call;
The freshness, the freedom, the farness —
  Oh God, how I'm stuck on it all!

The winter! the brightness that blinds you,
  The white land locked tight as a drum,
The cold fear that follows and finds you,
  The silence that bludgeons you dumb.
The snows that are older than history,
  The woods where the weird shadows slant;
The stillness, the moonlight, the mystery,
  I've bade 'em good-bye — but I can't.

There's a land where the mountains are nameless,
  And the rivers all run God knows where;
There are lives that are erring and aimless,
  And deaths that just hang by a hair.
There are hardships that nobody reckons;
  There are valleys unpeopled and still;
There's a land — oh, it beckons and beckons,
  And I want to go back — and I will.

They're making my money diminish;
  I'm sick of the taste of champagne.
Thank God! when I'm skinned to a finish

I'll pike to the Yukon again.
I'll fight — and you bet it's no sham-fight;
   It's hell! but I've been there before;
And it's better than this by a damn sight —
   So me for the Yukon once more.

There's gold, and it's haunting and haunting;
   It's luring me on as of old;
Yet it isn't the gold that I'm wanting
   So much as just finding the gold.
It's the great, big, broad land way up yonder,
   It's the forests where silence has lease,
It's the beauty that thrills me with wonder,
   It's the stillness that fills me with peace.

Approaching Chilkoot Pass
Margaret Shand

Davy and I, like many others, made our headquarters at Sheep Camp. We paid two Indians to pack our eight-hundred-pound outfit up the steep, stony cliff to this point on the trail. We carried our packs and went on ahead. The Indians made a cache among other stampeders at Sheep Camp, which was the busiest, maddest place in the North the first year of the Gold Rush, in 1897. I'll never forget it!

Even Davy was upset by so much noise and confusion. We could hardly move for people packing in and packing out, coming and going, buying and selling, and combining outfits. Men who had never seen one another before became partners without consideration of personalities or temperaments — all that was necessary was that one must have seven hundred dollars in food or five hundred dollars in money.

The police, who knew the dangers of winter in this cold country, saw to it that there was enough to feed the wild people who were gold-crazy and on their way to the Klondike. I found it all very exciting!

Sheep Camp is situated in a canyon that opens into a basin-like valley surrounded by high mountains covered with snow. "A man told me it was the headquarters for the mountain sheep hunters at one time — that is where it gets its name," Davy told me. "It marks the last timber line on this side of the ridge. That gorge through the mountains is called Chilkoot Pass. It begins at Sheep Camp, then comes Stone House, the Scales and the Summit, thirty-five hundred feet. It's up there, Peg, where the police collect the customs, as it is the boundary line between Canada and Alaska."

Davy always found out about everything. I was interested as he went on to explain a lot he had picked up about this new country. "Owing to the necessity of policing the trail and rivers, posts were established every thirty or forty miles. It's good management, because it would be almost impossible for a person to enter the country at Skagway without being seen. Davy and I sat upon our outfit as we rested and talked. There was so much excitement we did not think of sleeping. The twilight was long into the night. No one went to bed, but slept when he could catch a few winks.

"Now, Peg," Davy explained, "the duties of the police are many: preservation of order, collecting of customs duties at Chilkoot Pass and White Pass, the regulation of traffic, and various other services in connection with the government. When we get to Dawson, Peg, at the confluence of the mighty Yukon and Klondike rivers — there is the Mounted Police post that has the supervision of all this new gold country.

"I hear it has not near the lawlessness that Alaska has. The British are a law-abiding people — well, more or less." He smiled as I had to laugh at his loyalty to his homeland.

The pass was already covered with snow. On the steepest part of the trail, between the Scales and the Summit, it was packed hard as stone. Some men had cut out steps and charged toll for their use. A continual line of packers came up the pass like a parade.

The first time Davy and I made the climb we had a terrifying experience. Davy thought we should not carry too heavy a pack until we got a bit used to the exertion of the hard climb. We stopped for breath. It was tough going, even if one did not have a pack on his shoulders. We rested. I looked up at the high mountains of Chilkoot Pass, looming above us. Ahead was a rugged, exhausting climb.

My pack did not seem so heavy when I started — Davy had seen to that. I struggled along, climbing, climbing, and it grew heavier until I felt I had the world on my back. The straps cut and galled my shoulders.

The weight and the climb put a strain on my muscles in a new place. Underfoot was rough going; my feet slid over the rocks. At times I had to crawl, using my hands and feet in a constant effort, lifting and pulling upward. Davy, too, had a hard time — I didn't complain for I was afraid he would tell me I should not have come. He was puffing and blowing worse than I.

It was hard to breathe. My heart pounded in my ears with sickening nausea. A tottering weakness shook my knees. I had to rest often. Davy was glad when I did, for he was almost worn out himself.

People filed by us in a continuous stream of the gold rush. It made me think of an army of ants I used to watch on the ranch. Everyone was carrying all he dared. Only the Indians climbed easily and lightly along the trail.

About two miles from Sheep Camp, at Stone House, a cutoff from the main trail runs close to the base of the mountain.

"Peggy, see that overhanging wall of ice?" Davy pointed it out to me. "It certainly looks dangerous."

We could see this glacier below us from our position on the upper trail. We were packing along slowly when suddenly there was an ominous rumble. It shook the ground under our feet. There was a terrific explosion, another, and then another, each one louder than the one before — a cracking, splitting sound as if the whole mountain were being torn apart.

"Look, Peg," Davy cried. "Look! It's an avalanche! It's breaking loose."

As we watched we saw a widening wall of water and ice crashing down the mountainside, sweeping everything before it.

"Davy, what shall we do?" I screamed. "We shall be killed. The mountain is going."

"Stand still, Peg," he commanded. "It's on the other side of the trail and below us. See those fellows running for their lives? God! I hope they make it."

They were tearing their packs from their shoulders to run the better. The packs fell in the terrifying, moving, slipping avalanche and were quickly carried out of sight. I felt as if the whole mountain were sliding out from under us. Suddenly it was over as we watched. The mountainside was swept clean. I stood frightened, weak and trembling.

After we had regained enough strength we plodded along until at last we reached the Summit. We were wearying and loosened our packs to rest a bit. Davy left to see about getting our outfit through the government customs.

Alone, sitting on my pack, I looked far away at the distant mountains, purple and majestic — over these we must climb. They were like a wall guarding a new world beyond. The sight gripped me. I trembled all over. Nothing in my life had ever frightened me like those snow-capped peaks. To struggle over those mountains meant going into a new land, a new life, like being born again. Just Davy and I! Were we equal to it? Could we measure up to this great challenge?

I can never explain the fear that shook the very heart of me. I wanted to get Davy and hurry down the mountainside, back to the things I knew, back home, back to Scotland and brother Jack and security. I was shaking with terror. I covered my face with my hands. What had we gotten ourselves into? I dared not look again at those mountains. After a bit I grew calm. I remembered experiencing this same strange fear when a child. One cold winter night Father had lifted me up on the old stone wall and told me to look at the stars in the heavens.

"No, no," I cried. "I dinna want to look. I 'fraid." I covered my eyes with my hands and hid my face on his shoulder.
"Never be afraid of anything, lass," he told me. "You can never lose the stars, lassie; they are always in the sky, just as God is always with you. Mind this."

I opened my eyes now and looked at the mountains. My father's voice came back to me, as he read at family worship: "I will lift up mine eyes unto the hills from whence cometh my help. Suddenly a great strength and power possessed me. I felt equal to any trial that might come. A golden light shone about and within me. My heart prayed, "Oh, God, show me what to do, and give me strength to do it."

When Davy returned he looked at me twice and said, "Well, Peg, what happened? You don't look like the tired gir-rul I left here. You seem all rested." I couldn't tell Davy about it just then, but I shall never forget this experience on Chilkoot Pass, when I gazed in awe at the summit and beyond.

It soon became necessary to contrive a better way to get the outfit over the steep trail to the summit. A company of men fixed a trolley by running a long rope through a sheave anchored at the summit one attached to a drum and the other to the loaded sled. The drum was wound by horsepower. It proved a satisfactory contrivance to transport the goods to the summit. For a good price, a person saved himself a lot of hard packing.

To the right of Chilkoot Pass was the Patterson Trail, longer and more gradual. This was used for freighting. Horses, dogs, oxen, tame elk, goats, or anything that could pull a load up to the Waterways, was used for the purpose.

We worked hard to get our outfit up to Crater Lake. Here we made our cache on the mountainside, along with others. It was now October and getting very cold. Traveling over the trail so often, we grew to know those who, like ourselves, were packing in. I talked little to strangers. Davy stopped to chat and hear the news. I stood beside him, listening. The Indian packers grew to know me and called me "Little White Bird." I never knew why this name. One time, when I was resting by myself, an Indian said to me, "Hurry! Hurry! Get outfit cached up lake. Very soon, very cold! Little White Bird and man too late. Every day snow come down more, more, from high mountain cover trail. Wind howl. Sagna, home of North Wind, live in high mountain. He howl all time." Looking up, he waved his arm toward the snow-capped peaks where the North Wind lived. "Little White Bird no go all snowed in." He shifted his pack, grinned at me, and trotted down the trail.

There were many interesting things happening along the trail; some of them amused me a great deal. I saw a man pay five dollars for a cup of coffee. I thought that if it had been a cup of tea, there might have been some sense in it. I heard two men talking. One said to the other, "I just gave a fellow eight dollars for a pound of tobacco." His partner was shocked.

"You don't mean to tell me you gave all that money for just tobacco! It must be mighty good tastin'. I never chewed myself, but if it's that good, think I'll get myself some." And he did.

One cold, foggy day, when we were packing up to the Summit, Davy had a cold and was feeling weak. He stumbled and almost fell backwards. A young man who was just behind caught Davy. They got to talking. We asked him to share our lunch and he accepted. We often met the lad on the trail after this, as he, too, was packing up to Lake Lindeman. Though he was a rough looking fellow, Davy took a great fancy to him and it grew into a nice friendship. He was one of the kindest men we met along the trail. Always full of fun, we were glad when we saw him. In later years he visited us on Stewart Island. He sent us one of the first books he published. Davy was very proud of it. His name was Jack London.

One cold morning we were nearing Stone House when we came upon six dead horses. It was a strange sight to see them lying in a circle, as if they had their heads together for comfort in their misery. They had died from exposure, abuse, and starvation. In place of the backbreaking loads, the terrible pull up the mountainside, the weakness from hunger and the chill of the icy wind, they were mercifully released from their suffering. One of the strange sights of the trail. We never knew why they died in this way.

The way the animals were abused on the Patterson and other trails is too horrible to think about. I often told Davy, "All the gold in the country is not worth this cruelty."

It became necessary to make greater haste in packing up to Crater Lake over Long Lake to Lake Lindeman. We must get the outfit to the Waterways before the big freeze-up. We heard the old prospectors and others who knew this northern country talk of the long, cold winter. We must reach the Klondike and get fixed as comfortably as possible before the winter set in.

On the way from Crater Lake a blizzard struck us. The dark sky opened up and pelted us with blinding snow that stung like birdshot. The wind howled and screamed like a banshee. It was terrifying. We could understand why the Indians believed that storm demons lived in the mountains.

The wind tore about us, tugging at our clothes and hissing in our ears. The thick, slanting barrage of snow shut out the light. Even when only a few feet from one another, the white gloom completely concealed us.

"Peg, stay close by," Davy shouted. "Don't get separated from me. I must find the markings of this trail. There is an old boat turned upside down; we slide down into the canyon from there. For God's sake, don't get lost. You know how you are, always taking the wrong direction. You might get out on the lake. Can't tell how far it's frozen out there. You'd go down into the water—that would be the end. Stay close by."

"I will, Davy," I promised. I twisted about to straighten my clothes that were tugging about me and to adjust my pack. In that second I lost sight of Davy. Squinting into the blizzard I shouted with all my might: "Davy! Davy! I don't see you! Answer me, Davy!" But Davy was trying to find the markings of the trail. I heard him call to me above the howl of the storm:

"Come on gir-rul! Keep close and don't be idling."

"But Davy, I can't find you!"

In one hand I carried a bucket in which I had packed a bit of tea, sugar, dried meat and hardtack. A candle, and little odds and ends I had learned by experience to always have with me. In the other hand was my precious valise. On my shoulders were my blankets.

"Oh, Davy!" I screamed, "I'm lost!"

The blinding storm shrieked and I cried again and again into the face of it. "Davy, oh, Davy, come to me."

Davy, burdened by an eight-by-ten tent, by ridgepole and blankets, could hardly stand in the terrific wind. While struggling with the gale, I stumbled and fell. As I tried to get to my feet, I touched a slippery surface and knew I was out on the lake. For a moment panic gripped me; I was sick with horror.

"Davy, Davy!" I shouted frantically. The wind seemed to force the words back into my mouth. I thought of the tales I had heard of men frozen to death before they realized what was happening. I struggled to my feet. The snow had sifted into my mittens when I fell, but I knew I must not let go of the bucket of food and the precious valise.

Each step I took might take me nearer to where I would fall off into space, and the black, icy water close over me. I was facing death. I could not die here all alone, drowned in the black water.

"Oh, God, help me find Davy!" I pleaded. Then I heard Davy's frantic voice through the storm: "Peg, Peg, lass! Oh, Peg!"

"Davy, come to me!" I sobbed.

"Why did you do such a daft thing?" he chided when we were together again. "I told you to stay close by! Now I don't know where we are!"

"But everything is all right now, Davy. We are together again" I was breathless, but relieved and happy.

"I'm not so sure," answered Davy. "If I could only find that boat, then I'd know we were not headed out on this damned lake!"

"Davy, I know we're going in the wrong direction. We should go the opposite way," I argued.

"That settles it, Peg," Davy scolded. "Come on. This is the right way. You are always wrong about the way to go."

We struggled, weary and exhausted, I keeping close to Davy'. The wind grew fiercer. At last, just as we thought we could go no further, Davy found the boat. We both felt we had been reprieved from almost certain death.

Crater Lake is the bed of an extinct volcano and its banks are steep. The distance into the canyon from the lake was a hard climb even in pleasant weather, but in a blinding blizzard it was next to impossible to accomplish.

Davy surveyed the situation and then said, "Now I will slide down, and then when I am ready, you must come as I tell you."
I could hardly see him as he worked his way down the steep incline. I waited until I heard his voice and knew he was safe at the bottom.

"Throw me down your things," Davy called. I tossed my valise and Davy caught it.

"Davy, be careful of the bucket," I cautioned. "It's a good thing I tied the cloth over the top so the things won't fall out."

"Now, come on, gir-rul," he ordered. I slid down and landed in a big snowdrift where I lay, spent and exhausted, unable to pull myself out. Davy struggled to me.

"Ah, Peg, gir-rul," he grieved. "I never thought I'd bring you to this when I married ye." He put his arms about me and tried to pull me to my feet. After a time we found our belongings and again got the burdens adjusted to our weary shoulders. The storm grew worse and the cold more deadly.

"Peg," Davy gasped. "I think we had better put up our tent. We can't go on; we're too tired."

"No, Davy!" I screamed above the hiss of the storm. "We couldn't get the tent up in this tearing wind, and there is no way to make a fire. We'd freeze without one. We're above the timber line and no way to find wood to burn. We'd better go on. Better keep moving. We'll find the trail and get back to the Summit," I urged. But Davy's strength was fast deserting him.

"Peg," he moaned, "I can't make it." He sank down in the snow.

"Oh, Davy, please don't faint!" I pleaded, struggling to his side.

"Wake up! Open your eyes!" In the dim light, through the whirling snow flurries, I could see him fade from me. A ghastly blue came over his face. I shook him desperately. "Wake up, Davy!" I begged. "We can't freeze. Oh, God, help me save Davy."

But the only answer was the fierce, desolate howling of the wind. Suddenly through me flashed the same strength I had felt the first time I climbed Chilkoot Pass. I must save my husband! I didn't know how, but I knew it could be done!

Peering through the slanting sleet, I could make out a faint star close to the horizon in the distance. I realized, suddenly, that it wasn't a star. It was a light shining—the light from the open flap of a tent as someone went in. If we could only get to the tent and blessed warmth! I pulled the pack from Davy's back and piled all our things together and stuck the ridgepole in the snow above them so that we could find them later. Then together we dragged ourselves to the tent from which the light had come.

"How is it for getting in, boys?" Davy called out in a trembling voice. Voices came from the canvas walls: "No chance, no room; all filled up; ten men in here now."

"But we must come in. My wife is nearly frozen," Davy called.

"What! You have a woman with you?" somebody asked.

"Yes, we're lost; we lost the trail on Crater Lake," Davy answered. The flap was thrown back and Davy and I were welcomed into the shadowy tent, where the flickering light of candles showed a blur of faces in the cloud of steam from wet blankets. A fire was burning in a small Yukon stove, and the air, mingled with the body heat of the men, was heavy and hot.

Kind hands led me to a pile of brush that had been gathered for fuel to keep the little stove roaring. Here we rested and were given a cup of hot tea. I sat on a pile of brush and Davy leaned against my knees. I was happy to have him close, to be out of the storm, to be safe!

A wave of contentment came over me. My heart was filled with peace and happiness. I wanted to stay awake all night so that I could continue to realize, consciously, that we were safe. I begrudged myself the sleep that now and again closed my tired eyes.

I would nod and awaken suddenly to hear the storm still shrieking. In my heart was a prayer of gratitude that Davy and I were away from the terror of the wind.

The men were telling of adventures in other lands where gold had been found. Each man had his own experience to relate about what had happened in Africa, Australia, India, China, California. I wished Davy was not so tired and could tell them of his adventures in South America, of the engineering job he had superintended in the high Andes. I wanted these men to know that Davy, too, had traveled and had accomplished things before he became sick.

The night passed and when morning came the storm was still raging with no sign of abatement. Davy wanted to go out and find our tent so that we could have a shelter of our own.

"Davy, I can't bear to see you go alone," I insisted. "I must go with you."

But the men would not let me go out into the storm. Several of them offered to go. While they were gone I helped the owner of the tent prepare hot tea, hardtack and dried meat for the men. Davy and his companions erected the tent and we moved in, but our privacy was short-lived. We were no sooner in than four men came, asking for shelter. These men were packing merchandise and government supplies for the Mounted Police at Lake Lindeman, and they, too, had lost the trail.

"May we come in out of the storm?" they begged. "Well, we can't see you freeze," Davy answered.

They all managed to squeeze into our tent. The men were hungry and lost no time in preparing some food. Two of them rustled brush to burn, and the wind-swept tamarack and juniper bushes made a hot fire. One of the men had a little Yukon stove, another a bag of flour. Two of them were packing a hundred-pound firkin of butter apiece. The flour sack was opened by making a round hole in the top. In this hole, pancake batter was made of melted snow and baking powder, using what flour was needed without spoiling the rest. A firkin of butter was opened and a generous slab shaved off for baking and for spreading on the finished pancakes. My tea, sugar, and other useful things came out of the bucket to contribute to a fine meal for the hungry travelers.

I thought, "It's remarkable how little one can manage to get along on and still fare very well."

After eating the good supper, they made their beds in their blankets and then talked long into the night of politics, travel, mining, and of gold being found in the Klondike. One of the men told of his home in California and bragged about the fine bread their

Chinese cook could bake. He gave us the details of the baking, even to mixing in a cup of boiled rice, while I listened and followed each step. I had never baked a loaf of bread in my life, but now I felt sure I could do it.

Davy and I crawled into our blankets; I stayed awake to listen as long as I could, but soon I was lost in sleep.

I slept next to the wall of the tent. During the night my heavy braid of brown hair had escaped from under the blanket, and when I tried to get up the next morning, I found that it had become frozen to the ground. I pulled it loose and thought it quite funny. Nothing seemed to matter; I felt strangely happy and ready for anything.

Now we had to find the trail and begin the journey back to Sheep Camp. Although the storm was still raging, we packed our things and started on our way. The wild wind was so strong that frequently we were forced to our knees.

On the way we came upon a band of Indians caching their things under a tarpaulin. They were yelling and screaming, making weird sounds above the hiss and howl of the wind. I was frightened and wished I did not have to pass them. One of the packers told Davy that the Mounted Police were giving them double pay to show the white packers how brave Indians were to bring packs up the mountainside in the blizzard, but the wind was so fierce that even the Indians, who were accustomed to it, could hardly go on. Passing us, they dogtrotted down the steep trail, shouting and screaming above the howl of the wind. The storm and the shrieking of the Indians were terrifying and unearthly in the eerie green light.

Going down the slippery trail I could not keep on my feet. Slipping and rolling, I slid most of the way to the foot of the trail. But I held fast to my little valise.

At last we reached the Summit. The Indians had reported that a white woman was in the storm on the trail, and Major Walsh of the Mounted Police was waiting to meet us and took me to the barracks.

I was brushed free from snow, for I looked like an animated snowman. I was given a hot, juicy steak, the first fresh meat I had had for weeks. Davy went to the tent of a friend, where he arranged for a bed. Later he came to the barracks for me and found me rested and happy, listening to the police tell of their experiences on the trail.

The storm abated, but the white caps of the mountains seemed to close in. The Mounted Police sent out warnings that no more small boats could be used on lakes and rivers on account of the running ice. The big freeze-up was upon the land. Soon the only way to travel would be by the frozen trails on lakes and rivers. This was a great disappointment to Davy and me, for now we would have to stay in Sheep Camp all winter. What would we do for money?

Facing this problem was bad enough, but soon Davy came to me with more bad news. There had been a snowslide on Crater Lake, carrying everything away that was cached on the mountainside. A large cache of goods had been stored there for the winter, and our outfit was among them.

"Now, what will we do?" Davy asked. "The outfit's gone, and there's no hope of getting anything until spring. All we have left are the few things cached here at Sheep Camp. We have no money to live on, because things cost so much, nor have we enough money to go back. What will we do?"

"Davy, dinna ye fret; something will come up. We'll get through somehow," I told him, with a bit more confidence than I really felt.

"But where is the money coming from?" Davy wanted to know.

"Wait a wee," I said.

Later I heard two men talking. One said, "If I had known how to run an engine I could have had a good job. Cavanaugh at Sheep Camp offered to give me work at his wood camp running the engine to cut the lumber, but I didn't know enough about it."

I hurried to find Davy. Davy could make any engine run. He knew all about a job like this; he had done this sort of work in South America. He was pleased to hear of it and hurried at once to get the job. Davy even got a place for me to help Mr. Cavanaugh's sister cook for the men at the lumber camp. I could at least earn my keep and we would be able to save all our money to get a new outfit.

All women are supposed to know how to cook, and a man offered me fifteen dollars a day to make biscuits and pies in his hotel. Davy was insulted. "I will not allow my wife to work as long as I am able to care for her," he said.

I never forgave Davy for spoiling my chance to make all that money. However, I did not know how to make either biscuits or pies at that time, but I was sure I could learn.

The Golden Stair

The most memorable image of the Klondike Gold Rush is that of a line of stampeders climbing the Golden Stair. The throng of anxious stampeders toiling under their enormous packs and cases underscores the grim reality of their undertaking.

In total the Chilkoot trail is thirty miles in length and climbs 3,500 feet. The first third of the trail winds through coastal rain forest. The trail continues to climb gradually until it reaches Sheep Camp at the base of the Chilkoot Pass. From here to the summit the trail gains more than two thousand feet in elevation in less than ten miles. This is the Golden Stair.

The final push to the Chilkoot summit is a thirty-degree slope. In all seasons, snow slopes and steep ice cover this rocky gain. The Golden Stair had fifteen hundred steps cut into it, with a single icy rope to clutch to. Once a man stepped out of line, it could take him several hours to rejoin the trudge up the mountain.

Each stampeder carried almost a ton of provisions and supplies over the Chilkoot. This required each person to make an average of twenty to thirty trips along this trail. The wealthy could hire Indian packers or later in the rush use the tramway to carry supplies. Most stampeders simply put their heads down and grunted their boxes, bags and satchels over the pass. Many took several months to complete the Chilkoot.

The worst season to be in the pass was during the winter as sub-zero temperatures, high winds and blizzards stopped many in their tracks. The winter of 1897 – 98 was particularly harsh with more than 70 feet of snow accumulating on the summit of the Chilkoot. Overnight entire communities of tents and supplies were buried under mountains of snow. The Chilkoot was a dangerous place where horrible suffering was a daily reality. The worst disaster occurred on April 3, 1898, when an avalanche claimed more than 70 lives. Other snowslides also took lives. Creeks could flash-flood and take away a year's supplies in seconds. One flash flood drowned three men. The Chilkoot was a brutal, unrelenting pass, but it happened to be the best choice for accessing the interior.

The North West Mounted Police claimed the summit as Canadian soil and established a post. To maintain order, a Maxim machine gun was brought to this rag tag collection of canvas tents. The Mounted Police adopted the policy of turning back the ill-prepared and charging a duty to bring supplies into Canada.

From the Chilkoot summit to Lake Lindeman, the trail is entirely downhill. For most, simply dragging their supplies downhill was a welcome relief from the rigors of the Chilkoot.

Sheep Camp Washed Away
Tappan Adney

Next morning we follow the water from Crater Lake, a stream of some size, about four miles, past "Happy Camp — a misnomer, if ever there was one — until we reach the head of a lake, where there is wood and a little grazing for a few wretched horses. The wood is spruce, scrubby and sprawling, some of the trunks being a foot thick, but the trees themselves not over ten or twelve feet in height. There were about fifty tents at the lake, which is known as Long Lake, and is two miles long. We set up our tent on the spot where a party were camped who were just leaving, thereby having a few bare spruce boughs ready laid for our own bed.

The next day it begins to storm down the valley — such a storm as I never saw before. It blows until it seems as if the tent, which is held down by heavy rocks on the guy-ropes and the edges of the tent, would be taken bodily and thrown into the lake. Goods have to be piled end-ways to the wind or else be blown over.

The storm continues for several days, with wind, snow, and rain, the sun shining clear each morning through the rain. We engage some men to pack our stuff over, doing considerable ourselves. Now we see the need of the heavy shoes; anything less heavy would have been cut in pieces by the bare, hard rocks.

Having waited several days in vain for the boat to come over the summit, we start back to Sheep Camp, and on the way we hear that Sheep Camp has been washed entirely away, and many persons lost. At Stone House the square stone is gone. Several parties camped there tell us the first they heard was a roar, and, looking across the valley, saw a stream of water and boulders coming off the mountain top, the boulders leaping far out in air as they tumbled down, an immense torrent, and it poured into the Dyea River, overwhelming a young man who had gone to the river for water, undermining the big rock, flooding the tents, carrying away several outfits, and speeding towards Sheep Camp, bearing trees and wood with it. Sheep Camp, when we reach there, is a spectacle. The big saloon tents and many small ones are wiped out, and the main street, lately a trail of black mud, shoe-top deep, is as clear and solid as sand can make it. The catastrophe occurred on the 18th, at seven o'clock in the morning, before many were up. Numerous outfits were either buried or have been carried away by the flood. People are digging in the sand, wringing garments and hanging them out on the bushes to dry. Only one life is known to have been lost.

This disaster has decided many who were hanging in the balance. Whether they have lost their outfits or not, it has given them a good excuse to go back. From this time on only the strong-hearted continue on their way. Amid such general destruction I hardly expected to find my boat lumber, but it had been removed to a place of safety by the packer, whose feet had given out; but we find two men to take it over, and it accompanies us. I found among the wreckage a fine pair of Alaskan snowshoes, the toe of one broken off, which the owner parted with for $2. It is snowing as we again climb the summit, making the ascent both difficult and dangerous. The storm still rages at Long Lake. Tents are being blown down or are banging like the jib of a schooner going about in a three-reef breeze. Wondering if this is a permanent condition of the weather here, we start for Lindeman. The drop of eight hundred feet in elevation from Long Lake to Lindeman puts one into a new and smiling country. There are a hundred and twenty tents at the lake, half that number of boats in process of building, half a dozen sawpits at work, and a general air of hustle-bustle. In the words of the geography, "Shipbuilding is the principal industry" of Lindeman.

The ferryman at Long Lake refuses to go out in the storm, so we pay him full price, 1 cent a pound, for his boat, a large double-ender, load our goods in it, rig a small square-sail in the bow, and scud to the other end, leaving the owner to get his boat when the storm eases up. A portage of a few hundred yards to Deep Lake, and another ferryman takes us to the foot, a mile distant, where we set up tent.

The river here drops into a narrow canyon at tremendous speed, falling eight hundred feet in two or three miles. The trail strikes across a spur of the hill, striking the lake near its head. Lindeman is a beautiful lake, four and a half miles long, and narrow, with a towering mountain on the opposite side. At its head, on the left hand, a river enters, and there is timber for boats up this river. Vegetation is now plentiful, but it consists mainly of willows and a dwarf cornus, or "bunch-berry," which at this season, with its purple-red leaves covering the whole ground, gives a rich look to the landscape. We pitch tent in a lovely spot, on which we decide to build our boat. We pack our goods over from Deep Lake, and when the lumber arrives we build "horses" and set to work constructing the bateau. We find some burros here of the Leadbetter outfit. Only three, hardly bigger than sheep — and how slow! Dr. Sugden is driving them when we first see them. The little beasts, trained at packing ore in the mountains of California, know how to go around the trees with their packs, but they are helpless in the muddy places, which alternate with the rocks. We take them for one day; but Brown says he can pack faster on his own back, so we let the next man have them. Every one is in a rush to get away. Six to ten boats are leaving daily. They are large boats, with a load of five to ten men each. The boats are of several kinds. A fleet of seven large bateaux got off as we arrived, but the favorite and typical boat is a great flat-bottomed skiff, holding two or three tons; in length over all, twenty-two to twenty-five feet; beam, six or seven feet; sides somewhat flared; the stern wide and square; drawing two feet of water when loaded, with six to ten inches freeboard; rigged for four oars, with steering-oar behind. Some of this type were thirty-five feet in length. There are several huge scows. Well forward, a stout mast is stepped, upon which is rigged, sometimes, a sprit-sail, but usually a large square-sail made generally from a large canvas tarpaulin.

A party usually sends two men ahead to build the boats. They must go either five miles up the river just spoken of and raft the logs down here, and construct saw-pits, or else to a patch of timber two miles back, and carry the lumber all that distance on their shoulders. A saw-pit is a sort of elevated platform, ten or twelve feet high. On this the log to be sawn is laid, and a man stands above with the whip-saw, while another works the lower end, and in this way they saw the logs into boards. The boards are small, rarely more than nine or ten inches in width. It is a poor quality of spruce, soft and "punky," and easily broken. There is some pine. The boards are an inch thick, and planed on the edges. After the boat is built the seams are calked with oakum and pitched. The green lumber shrinks before it gets into the water, so that the boats as a rule leak like sieves, but the goods rest upon slabs laid upon the bottom cross-ribs. Everybody is happy, singing at his work. When a boat is ready to be launched every one turns in to help, for some have to be carried some distance to water. And when a boat departs it is with shouts of good wishes and a fusillade of revolver-shots. Nails are in great demand, bringing $1 or more a pound; likewise pitch, which commands the same. A few days ago, in order to finish a boat, a man gave $15 for two pounds of pitch. No one will sell lumber at all. Many are selling out and going back even after reaching here.

The last of September it snowed six inches, and it continued to snow a little each day after that. We had to work under an awning. At Crater Lake there were said to be snowdrifts twenty feet deep. Still the people were coming, it being estimated that there were a hundred outfits on the trail this side the summit, as compared with two hundred and twenty-five two weeks before.

No one knows where Jim is. Three of my horses have been taken over the summit and are working on this side. The burros are feeding on rolled oats. During the day we had them they dined off flapjacks; but this is very expensive horse-feed. Forty cents a pound packing is added to the price of all commodities here. There are many selling out flour at $20 a pack. L'Abbé here throws in the sponge. The little French baker, Richards by name, from Detroit, true to his determination, is here with goods, having been working from daylight to dark, and even Simpson, with his newspapers. He is putting his canvas canoe together with alder frames.

There are but few of the *Islander* party this far. I see only the Beall and Bowman party. A few are ahead, but the rest are behind or on the Skagway trail.

I was laid up for a week — the constant wet and cold had been too much. Work stopped on our boat. On the 4th of October the snow went off. On October 5th our boat is finished; we had decided to remodel her, giving her six inches more width top and bottom. The last seam is calked today, and she is carried down to the lake, and the next day we load the goods into her. She stands 23 feet over all; 6 feet beam; 16 feet by 30 inches bottom; draught, 18 inches with 1500 pounds of cargo.

We start amid a salvo of revolver-shots. The lake is as smooth as glass — what Brown calls an "ash breeze." So he gives her the ash oars until a real breeze springs up, when we hoist a sprit-sail, and in a short while are at the foot of the lake, where several other boats are about to be lined through a nasty thoroughfare into Lake Bennett. It has raised a great load of anxiety from our minds that our little boat carries her load so well; above all, even when loaded she responds to the oars in a way that delights Brown.

While we are unloading, a man leading some horses with packs comes down the bank of the lake. There is something familiar about him. A second glance reveals John B. Burnham, of Forest and Stream, whom I supposed still on the Skagway trail, and tell him so, whereupon I discover that here, at Lindeman, is the end of the Skagway trail! Thirty-one miles from Dyea via Chilkoot; forty-five miles from Skagway via White Pass.

Burnham's party of five, seeing that all could not get through, have undertaken to put two through with full outfits, and this is the last load. Burnham and another are to undertake the journey in four canvas canoes, two canoes being loaded as freight-boats and taken in tow.

The opening of the White Pass as a summer trail was not a blunder — it was a crime. When the British Yukon Company was advertising the White Pass trail and booming its town-site and railway proposition, the trail was not cut out beyond the summit of the pass. There was at that time no trail, and there has been since no trail, but something that they have called a trail, marked by the dead bodies of three thousand horses, and by the shattered health and the shattered hopes and fortunes of scores — nay, hundreds — of men. Captain Moore, whose alleged town-site rights the British Yukon Company acquired, supposed the trail ought to come out at the Windy Arm of Tagish. The exploration party of the Canadian government, proceeding by the natural course, went by way of Touchi Lake into Taku Arm of Tagish, and, in consequence of their belief that that was the trail, have established the custom-house at the outlet of Tagish.

The story of the Skagway trail will never be written by one person. It is a series of individual experiences, each unique, and there are as many stories as there were men on the trail. How much of the awful destruction of horses was caused by the trail, and how much by the ignorance and cruelty of the packers, will never be known.

One outfit killed thirty-seven horses, and there were others that equaled or surpassed that figure. On the other hand, a Black Hills man, no other than he of the buckskins, at whom some smiled aboard the steamer, packed alone with three horses twenty-four hundred pounds from the "Foot of the Hill" to Bennett in eighteen days. Each night, no matter how tired, he put his horses' feet in a bucket of water, washed the mud off their legs and dried them, and washed their backs with salt water. He came through when the trail was at its worst, and sold the horses at Bennett for a fair sum.

The attempt to blast the rock out of the trail ended in a fizzle. The giant-powder ordered from Juneau went back unused. The only real work was done by the miners themselves in corduroying. Half-way in on the trail goods were actually given away, the unfortunate owners having neither money nor strength to pack them either ahead or back, and the trail being in such terrible condition that outfits not only had no sale value, but could hardly be accepted even as a gift. At Lindeman comparatively few boats have been sold, each party generally building its own. At Bennett, however, there is a sawmill, and boats have been built by contract, the prices ranging from $250 to, in certain instances, as high as $600. Passage to Dawson is $50 light; with small outfit, $125.

Chilkoot Pass

Margaret Shand

During the winter, while Davy was running the sawmill engine, I was helping cook and learning a great deal about cooking, and earning my board besides. Miss Cavanaugh and I had a lot of fun; there was always something to laugh about. There was a young woman sent out by an Eastern newspaper to write up the gold rush, and she liked to enter into our good times. We three set out one afternoon to go to the Summit. As usual, I carried my little valise.

"Why do you always carry that little valise?" the newspaperwoman asked. "You must have diamonds in it."

"Not diamonds," I said, "but opals." I took the lovely stones out and showed them to her.

"Oh, my goodness!" exclaimed both girls. "Don't you know opals are unlucky?" they asked.

"Why don't you get rid of them?" the Eastern woman said. "Sell them, or give them away even."

"Shall I give them to you?" I asked.

"Not me; they're beautiful, but I wouldn't have them. I don't believe in tempting fate, especially in this country. One must be careful of one's luck up here. Everything depends on it. No opals for me."

We talked about it several times. Finally they convinced me the opals had cast their spell over Davy and me. Davy had had poor health ever since he was in South America. Then there was the ranch, and now the snow slide. The more I thought about it the more I was certain the opals had brought bad luck. I went out on the trail alone. I knew I must do something about it. I lifted the opals out of the valise and looked at them. They were full of fire; it was as if they were alive. For a moment I wondered how anything so beautiful could bring bad luck. But if they were responsible for Davy's poor health! Davy had never been sick as a boy; he was always so strong and well. I must not run the risk of anything happening to my husband. I had always loved the opals, but now I closed my mind to the lure of the jewels. At my feet was a hoof print of a packhorse.

It had been made in the soft mud, but now it was frozen into a little well, which seemed to me a suitable grave for these omens of evil. So I dropped them into the hole and covered them with stones. The opals were again hidden from sight in the dark earth! I was relieved and felt free of our bad luck and went back to tell Davy.

"That's just like you, Peg, to do a thing like that," Davy said.

I have thought that if I ever went back to that part of the country I could find those opals. I don't believe in bad luck now.

The last of March Davy left his job at the sawmill. He and I went to Dyea to purchase a new outfit. Though this one was not as large as the first, it was more practical. Living in the northern country had given us an understanding of its needs. We made arrangements to have the new outfit sent to Lake Lindeman by a company which was freighting goods to the Waterways.

Some of our first outfit was still cached at Sheep Camp and had to be packed over the Summit to the lake. We were working at this when the great snow slide of April 3, 1898, took place. This calamity occurred at Stone House, about two miles above Sheep Camp, where there was a cutoff from the regularly traveled trail. It was in this same place that Davy and I had witnessed a snow slide the first time we went over the trail. The Indian packers had warned the people of this danger, telling them that it was especially bad at this time of the year.

The heavy snow from the night before obliterated the trail, causing exceptionally hard going toward the Summit. Most of the white packers had quit and the Indians refused to travel, warning everyone against a possible snow slide. But some did not heed this warning and were caught in the tremendous avalanche of snow which roared down the steep mountain and choked off a long stretch of the trail. Sixty-three men and one woman were buried alive, under snow piled over them to the depth of thirty feet. The following day as we climbed the trail we looked down and saw some of the bodies being removed. Seven were taken out alive, but only three survived.

The sight of the snow slide disaster had upset me, so Davy insisted that I rest in the hotel at Lake Lindeman, a rudely constructed shelter, while he went back to Sheep Camp for another load.

I was resting when I heard a confusion of voices outside. Above the babble arose a woman's voice, crying and swearing. The man who owned the hotel was trying to quiet her.

"Woman," he ordered, "quit that cussing. There is a lady in here, so shut up!" This only made the woman cry harder and louder.

I ran out in time to see the woman pull a baby out of a dog sled. The child, so rudely awakened, joined its mother in crying. But after the mother had nursed the baby, it quieted down and went to sleep in my arms. The woman, too, seemed to feel better after she had eaten and told her troubles. Her husband had left her at home in the States while he joined the gold rush. She had determined to follow him. It had been a long, hard trip, and the farther she traveled, the angrier she grew. At the end of almost every sentence she swore vengeance, and threatened she would "kill him in cold blood."

The woman rested overnight at Lake Lindeman, and the next morning she started on her way in spite of advice to the contrary. She was a large, strong woman, and her anger gave her power to overcome bodily fatigue. The child appeared healthy in spite of the long trip.

I never learned if this incident ended in comedy or tragedy. I often thought of the poor little baby. In this country nothing was too bizarre to happen. I saw the first chapter of many wild tales, of which I never heard the ending.

Davy was returning back to Lake Lindeman when, on the trail between the Summit and Lake Lindeman, he was overtaken by a terrific storm, the last big storm of the year. The wind screamed and howled as it had done the time we were lost on Crater Lake. On this trip Davy was packing a sack of flour. He could hardly stand, the wind was so strong; he struggled on, step by step. The driving sleet pierced his face like steel needles. For days now he had been traveling with the glare of the sun on the snow. Suddenly he was struck by a pain in his eyes. He realized at once what this pain meant. He had seen men driven crazy by snow-blindness. It made them helpless, panic stricken.

Fear almost overpowered him. He was shaking so violently he could hardly make headway in the wind. It tossed him about and threw him to his knees. He crawled about on the trail, shielding his aching eyes in his arm as though trying to ward off the blows of devils. He must get up on his feet and keep going. He fought on and on, doggedly, with grim stubbornness. At last he realized he could carry the pack no further. The trail was familiar to him, even in the thick storm, so he left the sack of flour in a place where he knew he could find it. The pain in his eyes grew worse. Would he lose his sight entirely before he could reach me? Frantically he struggled on.

It was somewhat easier traveling without the burden of the pack. Mile after mile he stumbled along. Lake Lindeman was eight miles from the Summit; it was hard going, trudging into the teeth of the blizzard, and racked with the pain of snow-blindness. The pain in his eyes was constantly growing more maddening. When he finally stumbled into the little hotel he could not have gone another yard.

I had a man put up our tent, and we went to our own two selves. There I made Davy as comfortable as I could.

"Davy," I told him, "ye will get over your blindness."

I tried to comfort him. But Davy's suffering was almost more than he could bear. An ulcer was forming at the back of one of his eyes. The pain was so severe that beads of perspiration stood out on his forehead. I would hold his head in my arms for hours, and sometimes Davy slept this way, utterly spent with pain. Tears would stream down my face as I watched my husband who had always been so independent and sure of himself. Now I led him by the hand like a little child.

"Oh, your wonderful healing hands, how could I stand this pain without these hands!" Davy would say. "I hated to see you spoil them by helping to cook for those rough men last winter. God! How I hated it! You had never done work like that before. What would your brother Jack think?" Davy fretted.

"Don't worry about my hands. What does it matter? These hands are glad to work for you," I told him.

April and part of May passed, and Davy was in agony most of the time. I did not know what we were going to do. But never once did we consider going back to the States, even if there had been enough money for our passage.

We waited patiently for our second outfit to come up from Dyea. We had paid to have it packed up to Lake Lindeman. It must come. I had sent message after message about it, and had had one in return, to the effect that the goods had been lost in transit, but that the outfit would be found and sent on to us soon. Each day we watched and waited. I thought of going back to Dyea to find out about it, or make them pay for the goods. But I dared not leave Davy. He needed my care. A great fear gripped me.

"What will I do?" I thought desperately. Then there came to me a scene from my childhood. It was a cold day in early spring. The slush of snow was underfoot. I had walked with my father, mother, and brother Jack to church in Arnprior — as no one ever thought of taking the horses out on the Sabbath day. It was three long Scotch miles, and the old stone kirk was even colder than the snow outside. There was no heat, for such comforts were sins, frowned upon by religious folk.

I was cold and I snuggled under my mother's plaid and kept swinging my little feet back and forth to keep them warm. In spite of the cold I felt myself getting sleepy. All at once I heard the minister reading the Ninety-First Psalm. Jack and I had just learned it. I sat up and began saying it to myself.

"He shall cover thee with his feathers, and under His wings shalt thou trust — " On and on went the good man's voice. "For he shall give His angels charge over thee, to keep thee in all thy ways."

"'Angel's charge over thee!" I thought. "Why, if God sends his angels to take care of me, why do I have to be afraid? I never shall be again, for God keeps his promises. I won't be afraid of anything again."

I thought of the lovely white feathers in the angels' wings. I could cuddle under them just as I could under my Mother's plaid. A door seemed to open in my child's mind. Everything was all rosy and gold. For the first time God seemed real and close. His angels meant protection.

I felt this same protection now. I said over and over the Ninety-First Psalm, finishing with the plea "Oh, God, show me what to do, and give me the strength to do it."

At last the answer came to me. My mind was made up. I must go back to Dyea and find out about the outfit and get the medicine for Davy's eyes.

A man we knew was camped about a mile from our tent. I went to him and asked him to stay with Davy while I made the trip to

Dyea. I offered to pay him well and he agreed to take good care of Davy and to cook his meals. I then told Davy my plan. He thought he could not bear to have me go alone. He was afraid I might get lost, especially since the trail was more or less deserted at this time. He feared for me to go by way of the ice, which might be too melted and rotten. And then there were the bears, just waking from their winter's nap, cross and hungry. Davy was filled with fears — black, horrible, sick fears. He could not protest against my going, however, for what could he do? He was blind and helpless.

The distance from Dyea to Lake Lindeman was twenty-four miles. I prepared for the days I would be away, cooking as much as I could. I made Davy comfortable with our meager supplies and placed blankets over the ridgepole of the tent to keep out the heat of the sun, for it was hot during the day and the daylight lasted through the night.

The man I had hired promised not to leave Davy, but I was not sure I could trust him. As I made my preparations, I prayed over and over, "Oh, God, take care of Davy!"

Never in all my life had I found anything as hard to do as to leave Davy alone in his suffering and blindness. I leaned over him and kissed his thin cheek lightly. I did not want him to know when I left. He pretended to be asleep when I hurried out of the tent and commenced the long trek back to Sheep Camp and Dyea. My knees trembled as I ran along the trail. Over and over again I said my little prayer for Davy's protection.

I had set out at one o'clock at night, because it was colder then and the top ice, which had melted on the lakes and rivers during the day, would be frozen again so that I could travel on it. There were still a few more days before the breakup. Davy had warned me that the ice might not be safe. When I reached Long Lake, which connected Lake Lindeman with Crater Lake, I stopped to heed his warning. The ice looked safe enough, but there was a five-or six-foot stretch of water that separated the shore from the solid ice that bore the trail. I stopped to determine what was best to do.

Just then a man appeared. He, too, stood gazing at the ice.

"Wonder if it will hold," he said, as much to himself as to me. He was a tall young man with a kind face and a pleasant smile.

"My husband warned me not to try it," I said timidly. "He told me to follow the shore."

The man darted a quick glance at me.

"Well, I'll take a chance on the ice if it's at all possible. You know about the bears, don't you?" he asked. "They are just waking up from winter and I don't fancy meeting one now. Oh, I think the ice will hold all right. The part where the trail runs is the strongest of all and the last to go out in the thaw. I'm going to take a chance. I'll put my sleds together to make a bridge over this water next to shore and get out on the ice."

As I stood watching him I thought about the bears. The man now carried his goods over the uncertain bridge and then called his dogs. They picked their way daintily across the swaying sleds.

"Want to try it?" the man called to me. "If you're going down to Sheep Camp it's the quickest way. And it's safer than the bears." His eyes twinkled at me.

"Do you think I can get across?" I asked hopefully.

"Well, you'll have to take a chance." He smiled good-naturedly. "I'm due at Sheep Camp at a certain time or there's no use in my going, so I'll have to travel fast. If you are coming, come on. You stay about ten feet back of me and if I don't go in, it'll be all right. But if the ice gives, turn back and run like hell!"

Before we started he looked around and grinned.

"I've got on borrowed boots," he laughed. "It cost me seven dollars for the loan of them. If I get drowned my friend will be out of luck."

He hurried along the trail. I followed as close as I could, although keeping up with him and his dogs was difficult. The ice was covered with a slush of water which soaked my clothes up to my knees, but I did not have time to think about it.

The rotten ice held and I crossed Long Lake in safety. My companion was far ahead, but he waved his hand and sped on. Before I could reach the shore, however, I had to wade almost to my waist in icy water. I tried wringing the water from my skirt, but gave up and let it cling, wet and cold, to my legs as I ran along the trail to get warm.

Near the Summit there was an opening in the trail. I was startled as an evil-looking man came toward me. He had brazen black eyes and a drooping black mustache. He had fine new clothes and a heavy gold watch chain swinging from his plaid vest. He carried an overcoat over his arm and seemed out of place on the trail.

"Hello, there!" he greeted me as if he knew me. I mistrusted him at once. I knew no men of his type. Never before in my life had I feared a man. Never before had I been alone and unprotected. He came toward me.

"Where do you come from?" he asked. "Are you lost? Well, it's good I came along and found you all alone. How did you get all wet? Fall in?" he grinned.

He came close, ready to put his hand on me. I shrank back. I was frightened, but I did not dare show it.

"Oh, say now, you're a right good-looking gal. When we get you dressed up, some of the fellows will fall for you all right. I'm wait-in' for Nell Martin. She's to be along. She'll give you a job in her dance hall. She's to be here most any time. I been waitin' down there at the Summit for her. Thought I'd take a walk. Good thing I come along and found you."

I looked him firmly in the eye. I would not let him know how he frightened me.

"I must go on," I said. "Let me pass, please."

"Ah, see here." He stepped in front of me. "Don't you want the job? You're not afraid of me?"

My heart was pounding.

Just then, down the trail toward the Summit, there came shouts and cursing. The man stopped leering at me.

"Listen, what's that?" he exclaimed. "Guess someone's comin'. Let's go see." He started toward the trail. "Come on, sister," he called. "don't get scared — I'll take care of you. Don't try to run away from me."

I looked about. What should I do — try to run? No, I would not let him know I was afraid of him; and besides I could not run fast enough to get away, should he want to stop me. I would stand my ground.

A string of packers came along the trail. A fleshy, rawboned woman strode into sight at their head. The man went toward her, grinning. "Hello, Nell," he called. "I thought you'd never get here. Waited down there at the Summit. Come out here for a little exercise." The woman looked him up and down with bold, bright eyes. "Why didn't you meet me at Dyea? Afraid of an extra climb?" she jeered. "Well, I got here, but I've had a hell of a time, packing in all this stuff for the girls. Who's your friend?" the woman asked, eyeing me with cold, unfriendly eyes.

"Thought you might have a place for another girl," the man laughed.

"Looks a bit wet and bedraggled," the woman answered indifferently, and went on talking of her trip Outside.

As they talked, I slipped away. Just as soon as I was out of sight I ran with all my might down the steep trail. At last I reached Sheep Camp and went at once to the Seattle Hotel. Mrs. Card, who ran the hotel, was the sister of Miss Cavanaugh, the woman I had helped in the winter.

"What on earth has happened to your eyes? They look all washed out. I remember them as a dark hazel," Mrs. Card exclaimed.

The glare of the sun on the ice had caused an attack of snow-blindness and now my eyes felt as though a handful of splintered glass had been thrown into them. Mrs. Card treated them, dried my clothes, and made me as comfortable as possible.

The pain in my eyes was severe. I could not sleep, for I kept thinking of blind Davy and how terrible was his suffering. "Oh, God, don't let me become blind now!" I prayed. I cannot fail him. What would become of Davy if I did not get back to him? He had very little food and no medicine or tobacco. My eyes must get all right, for in the morning I had to go on.

Morning found my eyes sufficiently improved so that I could go on to Dyea. Here I found that the company which had been entrusted with my outfit was unable to locate it; but they were willing to pay me a part of its value. I could not wait longer to argue about it, for I must get back to my husband; so I accepted what they offered.

I was hurrying back from this errand and decided to look for a shelter for the night, as I felt I must rest before I began the long climb back to the Summit. To my chagrin, I came face to face with that man I had met. I was badly frightened, but made no sign of recognition. I wouldn't let him know I was afraid of him.

"Hello, there, sweetheart," he said flippantly. "I thought I had lost you. Glad to see you again."

I was in front of a small eating-house. I walked in and the man followed me. I asked the motherly looking Irishwoman back of the counter for something to eat, and inquired about finding lodging for the night. As I sat at the table the man seated himself beside me.

"Oh, come on, now," he said coaxingly, pulling at my arm. "I'll take you to a dance tonight. Let's be friends. I bet you can dance, can't you? Why don't you like me? All the girls do. Come on, let's get acquainted."

Worn out by a hard day on the ice and nervous from the attack of snow-blindness and shaking with fear, I could stand no more. The tears were very close.

"You wouldn't dare talk to me like that if my husband were here." I jerked away from him. "You let me alone!" I was so angry I would have struck him if I had had something to do it with.

The big, kindhearted Irishwoman, taking in the situation, came to my rescue and advanced toward the man with an angry gleam in her eye. He took one look at her and got to his feet in a hurry. Facing two angry women was a different matter, especially when one of them was big and strong and used to fighting.

"Now, you low-down trash, get out of here, and pretty fast, too! Don't you let me be a-seeing the likes of you about here again!" the woman said, picking up a chair.

He got out in a hurry.

"Now, don't you worry," said the good woman. "Come, dearie, you'll sleep right here with me and my family." She took me into the room back of the restaurant, and there she made me a bed on an old couch. I was safe, and warmed by the woman's friendship, I was soon asleep.

I awoke in the morning thinking of Davy and the long miles between us. This thought gave wings to my feet. The trail was greatly improved and I was able to travel with much less difficulty than the time Davy and I packed over it.

At last I reached Sheep Camp. I visited our cache and found things I had forgotten we had left there. I had to have help, so I engaged an Indian boy to pack it to the trading post. I determined to trade or sell the things for necessities. I had a rest at Mrs. Card's and then was ready to start.

Sheep Camp was in an uproar. A fire was sweeping up the canyon and the men were preparing to protect the camp. A pall of smoke drifted in on the wind and a sharp, acrid tang was in the air. Suppose the fire cut off my immediate return to Davy?

I had difficulty in persuading the storekeeper, whose mind was on the fire, to listen to me. But my necessity was so great that I lost all my shyness and insisted on his buying what I had to sell.

"But," said the storekeeper, "I can't buy your things. I might be burned out any time. Look at that smoke."

I paid no attention to his refusal. "If you can't give me money, won't you trade me some tea and tobacco for the things? If you get burned out you'll lose what you have in stock now anyway."

He thought that might be good reasoning, and accepted my things in trade for about ten pounds of tobacco and a large carton of tea. I bought Davy some medicine, new underwear, and a bottle of good liquor. I would not let the storekeeper leave until I had finished the trade and made all my purchases. By sheer force of will I made him help me get started, in spite of his interest in the fire. The Indian packer was loaded, and what was left I carried myself. I started on my way regardless of the advice of the excited people. The fire raged on, but I paid no heed to it.

At the Summit I had to declare the merchandise at the customs. Before doing this, however, I went into a place where I could get a cup of coffee. The proprietor asked me what I was taking in, and I told him some tea and tobacco for my sick husband.

"Well, you'll have to pay double duty on that tobacco if they know you've got it," he warned, and looked wise.

"Why should I be paying double duty on that tobacco?" I thought. "Davy needs it as much as he does medicine; and I must get it to him. No one shall stop me. Why let them know about it?"

I could not spare the money to pay double duty, having barely enough to meet our needs and get into the Klondike. I asked the restaurant keeper if I might step into the back room off his kitchen. I was wearing my suit of strong blue serge, and full bloomers underneath my ankle-length skirt and large balloon sleeves. Once before the big sleeves had been of use to me. They had filled with air when I fell off the horse into Dyea River. Slipping off the coat, I filled the large sleeves with small sacks of tobacco. And the bloomers, which had elastic about the knees, were filled with Star and Horseshoe

85

Plug. I was now ten pounds heavier.

When the proprietor of the restaurant did not notice any change in my appearance as I passed him on going out, I felt confident that I could pass the customs officers without attracting undue attention. I had to climb a long flight of steps to reach the Customs Office, which was built on high stilts to keep it above snow level. I started my ascent. I felt sure the police would notice my heavy load. However, up and up I climbed. What would happen if the rubber bands in my bloomers broke? Would the steps never end? They seemed mountain high. On and on I climbed, nearly stumbling in my fear and haste.

"They will just think me a fat old lady," I comforted myself.

At last I reached the Customs Office. Looking in, I was glad that I had hidden Davy's tobacco; for great stacks of money were piled on shelves, and on the floor in lard cans. Money every place. They didn't need our money. I looked the customs officers squarely in the face as I declared all my visible goods, including the tea. If the customs officers and the Mounties did suspect me of adding ten pounds since they saw me last, they did not voice their suspicions. I got my possessions past them successfully, waddling along, I made it by. The rubber bands held, and the Star and Horseshoe Plugs in the bloomers went down the long flight of steps.

With the aid of the Indian packer I now reached Crater Lake, cached my goods, and paid the Indian. Now that the goods were safe, I could travel the remaining eight miles to Lake Lindeman. The trip would take the rest of the night. The thought of bears kept me close to the shore along the muddy banks of Long Lake. I kept to the trail, sleepy, aweary, urging myself on with the thought of Davy and his happiness in receiving the medicine and tobacco.

Suddenly I heard a crashing of brush and a scuffling of padded feet.

My heart stood still for a long moment, and then it nearly tore itself out of my breast with pounding. There came a snorting sound, and a brown, hairy body about the size of a large hog, scurried on ahead of me. Snorting and blowing, the bear padded along the trail, and then turned off into the brush. In the violet light of the morning I saw him disappear.

I ran and ran, stumbling, falling, and picking myself up again, the

86

thought of Davy spurring me on. Then at last I saw our tent. I forgot my weariness as I ran in.

"Davy, oh, Davy, I'm back! And look! This is your medicine, and here is your tobacco!"

"Oh, Peg, gir-rul, you're back! My God, I thought — well, when you didn't come back, I thought...." But he never told me what he thought. Only his trembling arms about me told me what it had meant to him to have me back. His tears wet my cheek.

I laughed through my tears. "Davy, this is the thirteenth time I've crossed that Chilkoot Pass. And I'll say, 'I've gan no mere to yon toon!'"

It did not matter now that our second outfit had not been found and that there was little money. Nothing mattered; for now Davy could have his pipe and there was medicine for his eyes. We both laughed and forgot everything. We were together.

Paddle and Pray

Once over the Chilkoot Pass, the stampeders were still a long way from the gold fields. Boat-building towns were established on the rocky outcrops surrounding Lakes Lindeman and Bennett. During the winter of 1897 – 98 more than 20,000 people with little or no experience built 7,000 boats.

The landscape was stripped of its trees for firewood and planking for boats. The whipsawing of dimensioned lumber was the most onerous task of building these boats, and many parties split up as a result of fights in the saw pits. Once enough lumber was sawed, crude little boats were tacked together. The sound of oakum hammers filled the valley.

On June 3, 1898, the ice finally went out, and the most rickety armada ever seen set off for Dawson. The progress on the frequently windy and choppy lakes slowed many, but once on the Yukon River a swift current made up for lost time.

The most difficult rapids began at Miles Canyon, near present-day Whitehorse. Stampeders tried to find a route through a long series of waves in the steep-walled canyon. In the week after break-up, more than 150 boats were destroyed and at least ten men drowned. A short time later a tramline was built to haul boats and gear around this rapid. River guides also offered their services, and many of these guides were credited with more than a thousand safe passages.

The remainder of the trip down the Yukon River was technically less difficult, although white water such as Five Finger Rapids deserved careful consideration. The race to the Klondike was on, and in the midnight sun the stampeders paddled around the clock.

Miles Cañon
John W. Leonard

About twenty five miles, or a little less, below Lake Marsh, a wall of
mountains rises up, and the river, which has been about two hundred yards in width, is suddenly confined within a space of less than
fifty feet. This is the famous and deservedly dreaded Miles Cañon,
in which scores have been drowned. It is three quarters of a mile
long, and about half way down there is a sudden widening of the
channel into short curved bays on each side, then a contraction of
the cañon to its original narrowness until it emerges into the broad
river. At the enlarged center the rushing waters spread out and have
a terrific suction toward the sides, and then when the cañon narrows
again the waters plunge into the confined outlet with seething violence. Some go through the cañon safely, some attempt it and die,
and others take the only safe course and make a portage. As we
approach the cañon we keep to the right. If we decide to "shoot"
the cañon we lighten our boat of part of its load, use our efforts to
keep in the middle of the channel, and in about two minutes the
boat and its occupants will be through the cañon or else sucked
down in that powerful current. My advice is — don't!

On the right hand side, about one hundred feet above the cañon,
there is a smooth trail along a bench, which many hundreds of
Yukoners have used in making a portage. If we follow their example, three or four hours will suffice to get boat and outfit over the
trail, with everything safe and sound. It is a little work, but none of
the party is missing.

Keep to the Left
Our troubles, however, are not yet over, for having emerged from
Miles Cañon it is only between two and three miles to the White
Horse Rapids. Keep to the left! As soon as we reach smooth water
on the left bank we tie up and look for a place to make a portage.

Some run the rapids; but many of those who have attempted it
have drowned. The portage is not long and the danger to be avoided is equal to that just passed through at Miles Cañon. Near the

rapids there is a plane of rock, near the river, which is often used to line the boats through the rapids. This will do at a very low stage of water, but even then is dangerous. If the water is high, disaster is more than likely and many a boat has been dashed to pieces on the rocks or swamped in the waters when its owner has tried to line it down.

The best way is to make a portage of a hundred yards or so to safe water, and a little below is another stretch of equal danger around which a portage should also be made. It is about half a mile through White Horse Rapids.

On to the Yukon

The worst dangers of the journey are now over and the boat glides on, with a swift current, sixteen miles to the confluence of the Tahkeena River and then twelve miles further until we reach Lake Leberge.

It will be understood that we have been talking about the summer trip. Those who come in during March or April, before the thaw begins, will make the journey from Chilkoot Pass as far as Lake Leberge, if possible with sleds. They will then stop here, with the worst dangers of the journey past, to build their boat for the down river trip.

Lake Leberge is a very beautiful sheet of water, thirty miles in length and from five to ten miles in width. At its end we emerge into the river again, and after a run of thirty miles come to the junction of the Hootalinqua River. There are numerous rocks in this thirty miles, but after that it is plain sailing until at 135 miles below we reach the Five Fingers Rapids. For five miles before reaching them a marked acceleration of the current is noticeable. Keep close to the right bank and make a landing. If the load is heavy it should be lightened before attempting to go through.

Danger ahead

Five Fingers is an obstruction caused by a ledge of rock lying directly across the stream with five openings in it. There are four rocks of large size standing in a row across the river. If not too heavily loaded these rapids can be passed without any difficulty. Keep to the right.

Three miles below are the Rink Rapids. Keep to the right. There is no danger here, nor is there any more to the end of our journey. Below Rink Rapids we have the smoothest kind of traveling all the way to the mouth of the Klondike, which is about two hundred and thirty miles. We go on the first fifty-five miles, and the Pelly River coming in and joining the Lewis, we are on the main Yukon. The other important streams are the White, Stewart, Sixty-Mile and Indian Rivers, all streams of golden repute and then — the Klondike and Dawson City.

The Grand Canõn of the Yukon
Frederick Schwatka

On the morning of July 1st, we approached the great rapids of the Grand Canõn of the Yukon. Just as I had expected, our Tahkheesh guide in his cottonwood canoe was *non est*, until we were within sight of the upper end of the canõn and its boiling waters, and tearing along at six or seven miles an hour, when we caught sight of him frantically gesticulating to us that the rapids were in sight, which was plainly evident, even to us. He probably thought that our ponderous raft was as manageable in the seething current as his own light craft, or he never would have allowed us to get so near. In the twinkling of an eye we got ashore the first line that came to hand, and there was barely time to make both ends fast, one on the raft and the other to a convenient tree on the bank, before the spinning raft came suddenly to the end of her tether with a snappish twang that made the little rope sing like a musical string. Why that little quarter-inch manila did not part seems a mystery, even yet — it was a mere government flagstaff lanyard that we had brought along for packing purposes, etc., — but it held on as if it knew the importance of its task, and with the swift water pouring in a sheet of foam over the stern of the shackled raft, she slowly swung into an eddy under the lee of a gravel bar where she was soon securely fastened, whereupon we prepared to make an inspection of our chief impediment. The Yukon River, which had previously been about three hundred or three hundred and fifty yards in width, gradually contracts as it nears the upper gate of the canõn and at the point where the stream enters it in a high white-capped wave of rolling water, I do not believe its width exceeds one-tenth of that distance. The walls of the canõn are perpendicular columns of basalt, not unlike a diminutive Fingal's Cave in appearance, and nearly a mile in length, the center of this mile stretch being broken into a huge basin of about twice the usual width of the stream in the canõn, and which is full of seething whirlpools and eddies where nothing but a fish could live for a minute. On the western rim of this basin it seems as though one might descend to the water's edge with a little Alpine work.

Through this narrow chute of corrugated rock the wild waters of the great river rush in a perfect mass of milk-like foam, with a reverberation that is audible for a considerable distance, the roar being intensified by the rocky walls which act like so many sounding boards. Huge spruce trees in somber files overshadow the dark canõn, and it resembles a deep black thoroughfare paved with the whitest of marble. So swift is it, so great the volume of water, and so contracted the channel, that half its water ascends the sloping banks, runs over them for nearly a score of yards, and then falls into the narrow chute below, making a veritable horseshoe funnel of boiling cascades, not much wider than the length of our raft, and as high as the end of her mast. Through this funnel of foam the waves ran three or four feet high, and this fact, added to the boiling that often forced up columns of waters like small geysers quite a considerable distance into the air, made matters very uninviting for navigation in any sort of craft.

Every thing being in readiness, our inspection made, and our resolution formed, in the forenoon of the second of July, we prepared to "shoot" the raft through the rapids of the grand canõn, and at 11:25 bow and stern lines were cast loose and after a few minutes' hard work at shoving the craft out of the little eddy where she lay, the poor vessel resisting as if she knew all that was ahead of her and was loath to go, she finally swung clear of the point and like a racer at the start made almost a leap forward and the die was cast. A moment's hesitation at the canõn's brink, and quick as a flash the whirling craft plunged into the foam, and before twenty yards were made had collided with the western wall of columnar rock with a shock as loud as a blast, tearing off the inner side log and throwing the outer one far into the stream. The raft swung around this as upon a hinge, just as if it had been a straw in a gale of wind, and again resumed its rapid career. In the whirlpool basin of the canõn the craft, for a brief second or two, seemed actually buried out of sight in the foam. Had there been a dozen giants on board they could have had no more influence in directing her course than as many spiders. It was a very simple matter to trust the rude vessel entirely to fate, and work out its own salvation. I was more afraid of the four miles of shallow rapids below after the canõn, but she only received a dozen or a score of smart bumps that started a log here and there, but tore none from the structure, and nothing remained ahead of her but the cascades. These reached, in a few minutes the craft was caught at the bow by the first high wave in the funnel-like chute and lifted into the air until it stood almost at an angle of thirty degrees, when it went through the cascades like a charge of fixed bayonets, and almost as swiftly as a flash of light, burying its nose in the foam beyond as it subsided. Those on board of the raft now got hold of a line from their friends on shore, and after breaking it several times they finally brought the craft alongside the bank and commenced repairing the damage with a light heart, for our greatest obstacle was now at our backs.

The Cremation of Sam McGee
Robert Service

There are strange things done in the midnight sun
  By the men who moil for gold;
The Arctic trails have their secret tales
  That would make your blood run cold;
The Northern Lights have seen queer sights,
  But the queerest they ever did see
Was that night on the marge of Lake Lebarge
  I cremated Sam McGee.

Now Sam McGee was from Tennessee,
  where the cotton blooms and blows.
Why he left his home in the South to roam
  'round the Pole, God only knows.
He was always cold, but the land of gold
  seemed to hold him like a spell;
Though he'd often say in his homely way
  that he'd "sooner live in Hell."
On a Christmas Day we were mushing our way
  over the Dawson trail.
Talk of your cold! through the parka's fold
  it stabbed like a driven nail.
If our eyes we'd close, then the lashes froze
  till sometimes we couldn't see;
It wasn't much fun, but the only one
  to whimper was Sam McGee.

And that very night, as we lay packed tight
  in our robes beneath the snow,
And the dogs were fed, and the stars o'erhead
  were dancing heel and toe,
He turned to me, and "Cap," says he,

"I'll cash in this trip, I guess;
  And if I do, I'm asking that you
    won't refuse my last request."

Well, he seemed so low that I couldn't say no;
    then he says with a sort of moan,
"It's the cursed cold, and it's got right hold
    till I'm chilled clean through to the bone.
Yet 'tain't being dead — it's my awful dread
    of the icy grave that pains;
So I want you to swear that, foul or fair,
    you'll cremate my last remains."

A pal's last need is a thing to heed,
    so I swore I would not fail;
And we started on at the streak of dawn;
    but God! he looked ghastly pale.
He crouched on the sleigh, and he raved all day
    of his home in Tennessee;
And before nightfall a corpse was all
    that was left of Sam McGee.

There wasn't a breath in that land of death,
    and I hurried, horror-driven,
With a corpse half hid that I couldn't get rid,
    because of a promise given;
It was lashed to the sleigh, and it seemed to say:
    "You may tax your brawn and brains,
But you promised true, and it's up to you
    to cremate these last remains."

Now a promise made is a debt unpaid,
    and the trail has its own stern code.
In the days to come, though my lips were dumb,

in my heart how I cursed that load!
In the long, long night, by the lone firelight,
   while the huskies, round in a ring,
Howled out their woes to the homeless snows —
   Oh God, how I loathed the thing!

And every day that quiet clay
   seemed to heavy and heavier grow;
And on I went, though the dogs were spent
   and the grub was getting low.
The trail was bad, and I felt half mad,
   but I swore I would not give in;
And I'd often sing to the hateful thing,
   and it hearkened with a grin.

Till I came to the marge of Lake Lebarge,
   and a derelict there lay;
It was jammed in the ice, but I saw in a trice
   it was called the Alice May.
And I looked at it, and I thought a bit,
   and I looked at my frozen chum;
Then "Here," said I, with a sudden cry,
   "is my cre-ma-tor-eum!"

Some planks I tore from the cabin floor,
   and I lit the boiler fire;
Some coal I found that was lying around,
   and I heaped the fuel higher;
The flames just soared, and the furnace roared —
   such a blaze you seldom see,
And I burrowed a hole in the glowing coal,
   and I stuffed in Sam McGee.

Then I made a hike, for I didn't like
    to hear him sizzle so;
And the heavens scowled, and the huskies howled,
    and the wind began to blow.
It was icy cold, but the hot sweat rolled
    down my cheeks, and I don't know why;
And the greasy smoke in an inky cloak
    went streaking down the sky.

I do not know how long in the snow
    I wrestled with grisly fear;
But the stars came out and they danced about
    ere again I ventured near;
I was sick with dread, but I bravely said,
    "I'll just take a peep inside.
I guess he's cooked, and it's time I looked."
    Then the door I opened wide.

And there sat Sam, looking cool and calm,
    in the heart of the furnace roar;
And he wore a smile you could see a mile,
    and he said, "Please close that door.
It's fine in here, but I greatly fear
    you'll let in the cold and storm —
Since I left Plumtree, down in Tennessee,
    it's the first time I've been warm."

There are strange things done in the midnight sun
    By the men who moil for gold;
The Arctic trails have their secret tales
    That would make your blood run cold;
The Northern Lights have seen queer sights,
    But the queerest they ever did see
Was that night on the marge of Lake Lebarge
    I cremated Sam McGee.

A Dangerous Voyage
William B. Haskell

While I was acting as chief cook and woodcutter, and was making excursions for game in the country, Joe kept himself busy with the boat, and I helped only when it was ready for the caulking. It was finished in about ten days, and was a very good specimen, considering the tools we had to work with. I thought it looked small for the purpose of carrying our large outfit through very rough water, but Joe insisted that it was large enough, in spite of the warnings of one of the old-timers. Joe had been over the river as well as the old-timer, and he was satisfied. I was a fair swimmer, and I knew that I could get out of any place that he could, so I kept still. We named her the *Tar Stater*, in honor of Joe's native State. Every boat on the lake had a name, and one could see all sorts of clumsy-looking boxes carrying the names of all the States in the Union and of prominent men from George Washington to Grover Cleveland.

The ice continued to block the lake, being five or six feet deep in places, but the weather suddenly growing warmer, it broke and it seemed safe for us to embark. As we piled in our effects I saw that the boat was going to be pretty full, but Joe persisted that he knew what we wanted, and so off we started, working our way through the cakes of ice, and finding no very open water till we reached the lower end of the lake, which is about twenty miles long. Running out from it are long arms, the most prominent of which are Windy Arm and Taku Arm, reaching far up between the terraced and evergreen hills. The group lies in a depression between the coast range and the main range of the Rockies, and altogether it is a very picturesque region, abounding in striking promontories with a continuous fringe of wooded landscape along the banks, and back of them the impressive mountains seamed with little glaciers — gleaming like silver ribbons — while, breaking out here and there, little rivulets lead down precipitous heights and sometimes rose to the dignity of torrents. Mile after mile of wildest grandeur glides by like a continuous panorama.

At the mouth of Windy Lake are three small islands, and beyond them tower mountains of limestone and marble, and the beach abounds in marble of various colors. When we come to a little clear water we find it so transparent that we can peer to the bottom of the lake and see the fragments of marble scattered about. From the junction of Taku Arm, of which little appears to be known, to the north end of the lake, the distance is about six miles, and the width for the greater part of the way is over two miles. It is a fine piece of water, but apparently very shallow.

At the lower end the river issues from it and flows six miles to Marsh Lake. It is not more than 150 yards wide, and some of the way not more than six feet deep. On its bank, about one and a half miles from the lake, the Canadian police and customs officers are stationed. On the other side are the Tagish houses, or council houses of the little band of Stick Indians which wander about the lake country, and which, until recently, were not allowed by the Tlingit tribes to come down to the coast to trade. The buildings, though the only ones in the interior of Alaska with any pretensions to skill in architecture, are little more than rough enclosures, and the natives are exceedingly poor specimens of humanity. They have a simple way of disposing of their dead, and one of their burying-places can be seen from the river. The departed one is laid on a pile of dried logs which have been smeared with grease. A fire is then started, but the remains are seldom thoroughly burned, only charred, and over this they hold their funeral services, which are too complex for the civilized mind. It is their delight to go to a funeral, and when they are employed in packing for the miners or upper Yukon travelers they will, on hearing of a death, at once drop their packs and not return till the funeral is over.

A little distance below the Tagish houses is the entrance to Lake Marsh, so named by Schwatka after Prof. 0. C. Marsh of Yale, but most of the miners call it Mud Lake, though there is no good reason for such a name, and it is possible that it was originally given to the lower part of Tagish Lake, which is shallow and in places somewhat muddy. Its shores are low, flat and stony and the waters are shallow. The boat must be kept to the left bank. When we went through, it was still full of ice, though it was rapidly disappearing under the sun, which was now approaching its long summer course. Along the shores the vegetation was springing up as if by magic under its continuous warmth, while the rivulets formed by the melting snow and glaciers tumble over the rocks of the hillsides, falling in glittering cascades. The surrounding region appears low to us after what we have passed through, but it is picturesque in any season, the great terraces rising to high ranges on either side and not more than ten miles away. Prominent on the east stands Michie Mountain, five thousand five hundred and forty feet in height (so named from Professor Michie of West Point), and on the west Mounts Lorne and Lansdowne, six thousand four hundred, and six thousand one hundred and forty feet high, respectively. Wild fowl are plentiful along the flats, but nothing alive abounds like the mosquitoes, which begin to come up in swarms from the swamps.

The traveler finds the names of all the prominent features of the landscape of recent origin. Nothing more clearly indicates the newness of the country. Of course the natives have long had their names for the prominent objects, but they are seldom adopted by explorers. It is easier to go over the Chilkoot than to pronounce them as they pronounce them, for there is nothing in the English language sounding like their clicking syllables.

Near the foot of Marsh Lake a stream called McClintock River enters, and its valley is but yet little known, though it seems to be large, and it evidently pours in a quantity of the dirt that forms the shallows of the lake. The outlet of the lake is called Fifty Mile River, and it is here that the descent of the Yukon may be said to commence, though it is many miles farther before the great watercourse really begins. Here the water flows northwesterly through the great valley with a current of three miles an hour. From here on we had open water, and it was a welcome relief after working our way through so many obstacles. But in the springtime the banks of the river are constantly caving in and dumping trees into the stream, which is shallow in many places. Often we had to poke the nose of the *Tar Stater* out of the mud, for in many places the current seemed to run directly over these bars. The salmon struggle up to this point, and some of the largest are found here in season, but they never have the strength to get back, and in the summer large numbers of the dead and dying are found here.

After a rapid run down this stream, which twists and turns like a huge serpent in distress, the current becoming swifter and swifter, we came out into a wide sweep of the river where the water is still and gives little evidence, except a dull roar, of the dangers ahead, till the two frowning walls of the cañon appear. The river above the cañon looks about five hundred feet wide, and it is eight or ten feet deep. All this has to pour between two bluffs only about seventy-five feet apart, and rising in perpendicular grandeur for a hundred feet on either side. We found many boats along the west bank, and so we landed to take a look at what was before us.

Climbing to the top of the bluff, we gazed down upon the mighty current rushing in a perfect mass of milk-white foam with a roar intensified by the high walls of rock. The water was boiling through it at such terrific speed that it ridged up in the center, while along the perpendicular banks it whirled in huge eddies which had a very threatening look. The clouds of spray gave the water level a snowy appearance. The cañon is about a mile long, and while we stood there we saw several boats go through at the speed of a racehorse. But though they bobbed about like chips, they were generally managed cleverly, and ran through safely. By hard work they were kept in the middle of channel, but occasionally one would get to one side and be caught in the eddies and whirled around past all control. It was then a matter of luck if they went through without a mishap, for there was the greatest danger of their being dashed against the steep basaltic sides and smashed. But while we looked all passed safely through, though we could see that some shipped considerable water in the big waves.

"Pretty stiff gallop through there, ain't it?" remarked Joe as we turned to go down the bluff.

"I don't know what you think," said I, "but I know too little about managing a boat to run her safely through there. Besides, Joe, the *Tar Stater* is too heavily loaded to meet those waves gracefully."

So we finally agreed to pack our goods around. The portage path is over the east bluff, is about a mile long and the trail is comparatively good. This does not mean that it is easy. It leads over a high ridge just the length of the cañon and then descends abruptly with a dizzy incline into a valley, then, after continuing for some distance along the cascades, it ascends a sandy hill. It is very difficult, for many trees had fallen across it so that it resembled crossing a lot of hurdles. It leads much of the way through brush and wooded patches, where

103

the mosquitoes filled the air and made life miserable. One knows how to fight a big enemy, but a myriad of persistent little ones completely unnerve a man. On the first trip I took my clothing, bedding, and gun, and Joe took a one hundred pound sack of sugar and part of a sack of beans. This promised to be a slow process, and on our way back, as we saw another boat go through safely with a whole outfit in less time than it took us to fix a single pack on our backs, Joe began to get braver.

"I know the *Tar Stater* will ride as well as that coffin did," said he. Our boat was certainly handsomer than many that went through without mishap, but I still clung to the idea that it would not be well to try her till she had been lightened considerably. When we reached the bank again, we were approached by two men who were making it a business to take boats through at five dollars each. They wanted to take ours. I asked if she ought not to be lightened more, but after looking at her critically they said she was all right, indeed, was a pretty trim-looking craft. They had taken seven through safely that day, and seemed so confident of their ability that we made the bargain with them, and, as we must give them the same, loaded or empty, we foolishly decided to let them take her as she was. It would take two days to pack our things around the cañon, and as several of our camp friends had gone through we wished to keep pace with them. One of the men asked me if I would like to ride through, and I told them I would not mind if I should not be in the way.

"Jump in," they said, while Joe strolled up to the bluff to watch us.

We pushed off, and in two minutes my heart failed me, and I would have given all the gold I ever expected to get in these regions had I stayed out. Return was impossible. As we rounded the corner, and looked down through the cañon, I made up my mind that some fine work would be done if the *Tar Stater* went through those waves all right. I quickly pulled off my gum boots, thinking that if I should need to swim I would get along better without those, and then into the yawning chasm we shot, drawn by a force nothing could resist. There is a popular summer amusement called "Shooting the Chutes," very exciting and very exhilarating, I am told. A boatload slides down an incline, and splashes into the water. But just imagine a boat hurled along on a ridge of water running a mile in three minutes, and twenty times as long as your amusing chutes.

The two men started in to manage the boat cleverly enough. Not far from the entrance the boat seemed to take a fall of several feet, while all the waters in creation seemed to have fallen into a space seventy-five feet wide. The moment we struck the first high wave we shipped some water, at the second we shipped more, at the third it poured in around the whole outfit, and at the next we were full, and over we went into the ice-cold water with the worst part of the cañon before us. The boat turned toward the side I was occupying, and I sprang out so as to avoid being covered up. The moment I struck the water all fear was gone. It was easy swimming, for the current took one along whether he would or not.

When the boat came up she was about ten feet from me, and it was not easy to reach her, for struggling against the current was another matter. Finally I caught hold of the stern and climbed up. As I was swept by one of the other fellows, I got hold of him and pulled him in so that he could climb up, and a little afterwards the other man was able to reach us. There the three of us were riding on the bottom of the boat, which was whirling about in the wildest manner. As straight as a crow flies runs the cañon for an eighth of a mile. The roar was like a cannonade. On the top of the bluffs which flew by us grew dense forests of spruce which shut out the sun, and a weird darkness pervaded the deep and angry channel. The boat shot forward with lightning speed, leaping like a racer or bucking like a mustang, now buried out of sight in the foam, and now plunged beneath a terrific wave. We clung desperately to the bottom as helpless as flies.

A moment later we came to the worst place in the current, where there are three heavy swells, and where those who are steering boats through incline a little to the left to avoid the roughest part. But the current was steering us, and into the swells we dived. The waters swept us from the slippery keel as if we had been so many leaves. Again we struggled in the current, and again we caught on to the whirling boat, for after the swells the water became smoother, and in a twinkling we shot out of the cañon like a rocket, amid the reefs of boulders and bars thickly studded with drifts of timber. Two men were waiting at the foot of the bluffs in a boat, and when they saw us come out, they rowed after us and took us in. Thus we left the *Tar Stater*.

I had looked at my watch, which fortunately I carried in a rubber sack in my pocket, when I got into the boat at the upper end, and I looked again as we climbed into the boat which had come to our rescue, and saw that we had a little over four minutes of experience. Some of the boats go through in three minutes.

Wet and shivering, I sat down on a rock on the bank and felt very blue. Ten minutes before we had boasted the best outfit that any two men we had seen were bringing in; everything we would need for the next eighteen months. It was worth over $800, according to the way things sold in Alaska, and we had lost very many things which could not be bought on the Yukon. All we had left was the sack of sugar and a few beans; nothing to cook them in. We had no tent to sleep in, and we were two hundred and fifty miles from Juneau and five hundred miles from the nearest trading post down the river.

As I sat there Joe came down with a grim expression on his face. Joe had stood on the bluff and had seen us go under. He knew now that we had been too heavily loaded.

"The *Tar Stater* is down yonder somewhere," I said, with a despondent gesture towards the rushing river. I thought I would not be rough on the poor fellow.

"Well, the milk is spilled," he said, giving the forlorn bag of beans a kick.

"And this region doesn't flow with milk and honey," I added.

We walked along down the river, and about a mile and a half below we found the *Tar Stater*, bottom up, and her nose tucked into a crack in the rocks by the bank in such a manner as to be held fast. She was somewhat strained, and needed recaulking. We dragged her up to the rocks, and Joe looked at her mournfully. I could not withstand the temptation.

"The *Tar Stater* is a dandy in rough water," I said, and I could see that Joe was badly hurt. Then I was sorry and tried to make amends by saying that she would have gone through with flying colors had we only taken the precaution to carry part of the load around the cañon. "She is too trim for heavy work," I added.

On the next day a boat was overturned in running through, and two men were drowned. It was a sad ending to the hard voyage of two gold-seekers, but all along the river are the little marks which tell of similar cases. There were several parties camped at the lower end of the cañon, including some of the friends we had made at Lake Tagish. They were very kind to us, so that we managed very comfortably while we were getting our boat ready. This did not take much time, and having secured a set of oars, we loaded in all that remained of our costly outfit and proceeded down the river.

Below the cañon there is a stretch of somewhat milder rapids, or cascades, for nearly three miles, and then after a little smooth water we arrived at the White Horse Rapids, which are justly considered more dangerous than the cañon, but it is less on account of the swift current than of the formation of the passage, it being full of sunken rocks. It is, on the whole, the worst piece of water on the Yukon, and no one should ever attempt to take their outfit through. Of course, we were no longer hampered in this way.

In coming up to these rapids one must land on the west bank, which is formed of steep rocks, and the place is very difficult either for managing a boat, or for getting a burden up to the portage. Many drag their boats over the trail, but it is difficult work and requires several men to pull around in a day. To get the boats up over the rocks the miners had constructed a crude windlass. But most of those on the way with us determined to carry their goods around, and then shoot the rapids in empty boats.

We lined the *Tar Stater* down the side, and then went up to watch proceedings and to help one of the other boys down with his boat. We were gone some little time, and when we returned to our boat the sack of sugar was missing. I was mad. Some villain had stolen the most valuable part of the provisions we had saved from the wreck; that was about all we had left of that eight-hundred-dollar outfit. I strapped on my six-shooter and went hunting for that sugar with a vengeance. Theft is one of the worst crimes a man can commit in this country and it is not common. Only tenderfeet who have not outgrown the privileges of life in civilized regions will dare commit it. Generally, anything can be left with perfect safety on the trails, providing it is out of the reach of dogs. There are no store-houses, and traveling necessitates leaving articles of value all along the route. Traveling would be impossible but for a rigid regard for other people's property. It is the unwritten law of the land, and it comes as naturally to the Indians as to any one. Morose, superstitious, utterly ungrateful, and never to be believed, these Indians rarely touch a thing that belongs to any one else. They will leave their own belongings all along the trail, and they will be often passed, but no one thinks of touching them. They know they will be there when they return.

I knew it was some white man who had taken the sugar, and I went through the boats with fire in my eye. It would have been easy to find it had it been there, but it was not. On the other hand, everybody was in perfect sympathy with my attempt to find the thief, and if he had been found they would have given him, then and there, what, in the parlance of the Yukon, is called a "jig-in-air" at the end of a rope. It was lucky, perhaps, that I did not find him, for I was in a dangerous mood. I could have shot him dead and no one would have said a word against it. I should have been criticized if I had failed to.

Two or three boats had gone on through the rapids, and the thief had evidently taken the sack just as he was putting off, in the expectation of escaping safely. It would not have been so serious had he taken something from a party that was well-stocked with provisions, but taking it from us who had lost nearly everything but that, was sufficient to raise the indignation of the whole camp to the boiling point. The fellows offered us all we wanted. We suffered for nothing. We could make ourselves at home in any tent there.

There are some rare qualities in the rough breasts of the pilgrims of the Yukon, a consideration for the condition of others which is not always found in a softer climate and in an easier life.

There were, as I remember, six boats with ours at the entrance of White Horse Rapids, and we all went through in safety, but it was a thrilling experience. We were swept along over the raging torrent, which here and there throws white spray into the air, a fact from which the rapids take their name. The foaming waves seem to come from every direction. Ragged rocks hang over the passage, the current sucking in under them, and at times we could have reached up and touched the rocks with our hands had we cared to. We had too much to do for amusement of that kind. The rapids extend straight away for nearly a quarter of a mile, and then take an abrupt turn to the right. It is after passing the turn that the most dangerous part is encountered.

With a stream that is two hundred yards wide, full of ugly boulders, coupled with a fall of two hundred feet in five-eighths of a mile, it is no wonder that this stretch of river has become the terror of Alaskan gold-hunters. If the current in the cañon appeared to speed along with the swiftness of an arrow, that in the rapids seemed to equal the flight of a swift bird. The last hundred yards of the journey was particularly dangerous. At the spot called the "White Horse" the waters tumbled and tossed in a most fantastic fashion, piling up the spray in long white columns ten or twelve feet high. There is a sheer fall of nine feet at that point.

"Joe, we're goners sure," I shouted, holding on in terror. But the *Tar Stater* took the plunge in a way that gladdened our hearts. True, it seemed that we would never come up; and, when we did, it looked as though we would never come down. Into the air the bow went, and when the boat again struck the water flew over us in a torrent. We thought that the next moment would see the Tar Stater sink, but she did not. I think it was the swiftness of the current that kept her afloat. At any rate, we reached shore safely, but wet through to the skin. If anybody imagines that shooting the White Horse Rapids is easy, or pleasant, he is very much mistaken.

There may be some pleasure in boasting of having shot these fearful waters, but it is the height of folly to run the risk. Many go through safely in empty boats, but they are at the mercy of as angry a bit of water as there is in Alaska, and there are a great many such places. The summer before we went through, it was said that thirteen persons lost their lives there and all because they preferred to take the risk than to drag the boat around. It requires but a minute or so to shoot through, but days to get an outfit around.

Terrible as is the experience, there are few places more sublime to the view. Standing on the bank in safety, the eye is charmed by the water that leaps and foams around the highly colored rocks. You may watch it for hours and turn away with regret, and if the eye wanders off, it rests on the somber stretches of trees, in their varying colors, the luxuriant grass, and the tundra, while standing like ghostly sentinels over all are the snowy peaks in the distance. Everything is on a grand scale, and one acquires a faint realization of what this planet must have been in those untrimmed, uncut, glacial times when the earth was dotted with raging waters like these, and mammoths stalked or crawled about the gloomy hillsides.

Below the rapids the river flows swiftly on for several miles, much of the time between gravel banks, but the water is smooth, the banks one hundred and fifty yards apart, and no obstacles except bars appear; so we made good progress. The current becomes less and less as the river turns northward through the same wide valley. The bluffs along the bank are of white silt, which gives a cloudy yellow tint to the waters. About thirteen miles down we come to the mouth of the Tahkheena River, a muddy stream about seventy-five yards wide, flowing in from the west. Its sources are near the Chilkat Pass, and its waters flow through a large body of water named Arkell Lake, not far from the Dalton Trail. It is said to have been formerly used by the Chilkat Indians in reaching the interior, but now it is seldom used, though its waters are said to be navigable from the head of the lake down.

Our little party of six or seven boats kept close together as we drifted down the rapid stream, and, towards evening, as we were looking along the banks for a good place to camp, we came upon three boats and a little camp back from the bank. I had not forgotten the sugar; neither had the others. We disembarked with assumed indifference, but I immediately raised some consternation by going through the boats. In one of them I found a sack of sugar.

In less than a minute that boat and the man claiming it were covered with a dozen guns, but I was somewhat surprised to see my friends put a rope around his neck and lead him struggling towards a tree. The day before, when I was boiling with rage, I might not have said a word. I knew how heinous the crime of theft was considered in Alaska. But now I was somewhat taken aback by the swiftness with which my friends proposed to mete out justice. The man could say nothing. He was badly frightened, and those who had been with him on the bank made no protest; and, if they had, we were too many for them.

The rope was thrown over the limb of a neighboring tree, and a half a dozen men caught hold of it ready to pull.

"Hold on a minute, boys," I said. "It strikes me it's pretty tough to hang a man for stealing a sack of sugar."

"Hang the man who steals anything!" said one of the old-timers.

"But I don't want to be too cruel on the fellow," I replied. "He may know better next time."

The poor fellow was trembling like a leaf. His face was ghastly pale, and he looked at me with beseeching eyes.

"Wal, it's your sugar," said one of the men, "and all you've got to do is to say the word and up he goes."

"I won't do it," said I. "Settle it some other way."

"He's got to be punished somehow," said the old-timer, in a determined tone, "and, if you don't want to have him pulled up, you'll have to give him the lash. We sometimes does that."

"All right," I said, knowing that some form of punishment would certainly have to be administered.

So they made him take off his clothes down to his bare back, tied his hands together, and swung him up so that his toes barely touched the ground.

"Nothin' less than fifty lashes," said the old-timer, handing me a piece of rope. So I began to lay it on, and the more I did so, the more I began to think he deserved it. He stood it remarkably well, but finally began to cry with pain, and I stopped.

"Nothin' less than fifty," shouted the old-timer.

So I kept on till the number was reached. It was a pretty tough looking back he had when I finished, and he drew his shirt on with the greatest care.

I came to know that man very well later on. Strange as it may appear, we grew to be friends, and he made a good citizen of Alaska. I never knew of his again taking a thing belonging to another. These primitive methods of punishment are quite effectual, after all. There would be few burglars and sneak thieves in the States if the lash were used publicly, instead of the so-called enlightened method of retiring them to a rather agreeable life in a prison, to which they take their own evil natures, and where they exchange lessons in criminality with their prison associates.

Proceeding a few miles further, we arrived at Lake Laberge, which lies nearly north and south, surrounded by mountains, those on the southeast presenting very abrupt and castellated forms, with summits of white limestone. It is thirty-one miles long with an average breadth of nearly five miles. Its southern half is somewhat wider, but then it narrows down to about two miles for a distance of about seven miles, and at the north end expands to about four miles again. The western shore is indented with shallow little bays. Just before reaching the place where it narrows there is a large island, the southern end flat, with gravel banks and the other end rocky. The rocks are a bright red, and it makes a very pretty picture against the other colors along the shore.

The lake is about two thousand feet above the sea level, and we found it rough sailing most of the time, though the wind held in our direction. Its rough water is usually dreaded by miners, who sometimes are forced to camp on its banks for several days, till the wind goes down. The whole valley seems to be a great trough, sucking inland the southerly winds, which are apt to prevail in the summer months.

We made good progress on Lake Leberge, in spite of its roughness. Other names have been given this body of water, and the Indians have one of their own. Its common name is derived from one Mike Leberge, who not many years ago was engaged by the Western Union Telegraph Company, exploring the river and adjacent country for the purpose of connecting Europe and America by a telegraph line overland, except for the short distance at Bering Strait.

The days had become so long by this time that we could travel nearly all the time, stopping only now and then for a square meal. It will be difficult for anyone who has not been in the Arctic regions to form a good idea of the picturesque features of a sail along one of these lakes at this time of year. The shore of the large is fringed with a line of trees, which stretch back over the low hills, but over the tops of the tree towers the white line of mountains, miles away. And above these mountains is the canopy of heaven. Around this circles the blazing sun, hour after hour. One does not realize what a relief the darkness is till he comes to a region like this, at a time when there is no darkness.

On we drifted, over the ruffled waters, taking a cold lunch when hungry, but without an adequate realization of the time of day, unless we looked at our watches. Finally the sunset, and Venus was the only star which became dimly visible in the twilight of midnight.

About half way down the lake is a large bare rock where flocks of gulls make their home. Eggs are a great luxury in Alaska, and we laid in a supply as we could and feasted on them for several days. One can scarcely appreciate the amount of pleasure there is in instituting a little variety in Alaskan diet, for the appetite knows no bounds, and the staple food is extremely limited in variety. Besides, since the loss of our outfit we had been obliged to use our money to buy what stores the others could spare, though they were very kind, and would have given food at any time had we asked it. I kept my eyes on the shore most of the time, in the hope of seeing game, and although I found enough to provide us with many good meals, I could not fail to notice that it was becoming more and more scarce.

The Lewis river, as it flows out of the lake, is about two hundred yards wide, and for about five miles preserves this width, and a swift current of from four to six miles an hour. It then makes a sharp turn about a low gravel point, and flows for a mile in a direction opposite to its general course, when again it sharply resumes its way northward. Twenty-seven miles down we come to a great tributary from the southeast, the Teslin River, as it is now called, as it drains the great Teslin Lake; but the miners call it by its Indian name, the Hootalinkwa. Schwatka called it the Newberry, and Dr. Dawson had given it the name of Teslintoo; from which it appears that names in Alaska are sometimes uncertain, and time alone will tell which name will prevail. We were told by the Indians that gold could be found on this stream, but few explorations of it appeared to have been made.

The water of the Teslin is of dark brown color. Indeed, one cannot fail to notice, at least in the spring of the year, the amount of dirt these streams are carrying down. It is another feature of a fact that strikes a traveler at every point, the immense amount of work that Nature is doing these regions. The country in the section we have recently passed is extremely mountainous, with torrents plunging down through the rough valley from the eternal snows. The water in the lakes appears to be remarkably clear, but as soon as we touch any of the connecting streams we notice that they are so full of sediment that one cannot seen an inch below the surface.

If a basinful is taken out and allowed to stand until it clears, a thick deposit of mud is found at the bottom. The current boils and flows very rapidly and as the boat glided along a sound was heard almost like that of frying fat. It was only the constant friction on the boat of the immense amount of large particles of earth which the water was carrying in suspension. This is noticeable all along the river, and is an indication of the wearing down process that is constantly going on in this country. It furnishes the reason for the shifting bars which exist on the lower Yukon, and for the difficulties that prevail at its mouth. When time has done its work, the shores of Alaska, about the mouth of its great river, will be pushed out much further into the Pacific.

As we proceeded down the river we easily saw whence comes all this material. Along the silt and sand bluffs, loose material is constantly falling into the stream. These little landslides, occurring all the time, except in the months when everything is frozen, result in an immense amount of dirt being dumped into the river. We should be surprised if it were measured. I had read how Nature worked through countless ages, but I never realized the extent of the capability of the mighty forces, till I took that first trip down the upper Yukon region. But while we see Nature working in an earlier process than that to which we are accustomed, one is appalled to think how long she has been working even here. For all those mighty cañons which we have seen, and through some of which we have barely escaped with our lives, have been worn out by the torrents. These great rocks and boulders, which fill the stream and around which the swift current plays, have been rolled down from the mountains by the receding glaciers.

We found these huge boulders a great obstacle all the way down this part of the river. Sometimes it was all we both could do to handle the boat. The current would carry us against them before we could stop it, but we managed much better than some of our friends with loaded boats. Many of them bumped into the rocks, and one man lost nearly half his outfit.

About thirty-three miles below the mouth of the Teslin River the Big Salmon pours into the Lewis. Thirty-four miles more and we come to the Little Salmon, which is sixty yards wide at its mouth, and is shallow. Here the valley becomes so broad that no mountains are in sight, only low hills, at a distance from the bank. The Lewis makes a turn to the southwest, and after running six miles it turns again to the northwest; then, at the end of seven miles, to the southwest again, around a low, sandy point. Thus we proceeded for twenty miles or more, without gaining more than five in our northern course. The first turn is around Eagle's Nest Rock, which stands up on the slope of the eastern bank, and in it is a huge cavern, where it is said gray eagles rear their young. It is composed of light gray stone and rises fully five hundred feet above the river.

About thirty miles further on, another river, the Nordenskiold, draining a chain of lakes far to the westward, empties into the Lewis, which continues its course with a width of from two hundred to three hundred yards, occasionally expanding as it flows around little islands. Its course is very crooked, and near the mouth of the Nordenskiold it winds under a hill, and away from it several times, once for a distance of eight miles, and after making all these turns it has gained but a mile. From this the river flows on in a straight course to the Five Finger Rapids.

We did not stop to look at this place, but ran right in, and soon were bobbing about like a chip on the whirling current. It is a cataract of ferocious mien, but not at all dangerous, as a boat can be easily kept away from the hazardous points. As in the Grand Cañon, the water rolls away from the sides and is ridged in the center. Just before entering the rapids there is a whirlpool, which is studiously avoided, though it is not dangerous. If a boat got caught in it she is liable to be whirled about in it for some time before being released. The current continues very rapid for six miles below Five Finger Rapids, so-named because of the five large rocks standing in mid-channel, and then we began to hear the roar of the Rink Rapids. They make a great deal of noise, but are not dangerous, as the only obstruction is on the west where the water pours over the rocks. On the east side the current is smooth and the water deep, and a boat can run through without the slightest difficulty.

For fifty-eight miles, the distance between the Five Finger Rapids and the place where the Pelly River unites with the Lewis and forms the great Yukon, no streams of any importance appear. The river continues through a pleasant landscape for the whole distance without the slightest indication of civilization. About a mile below the rapids the stream spreads out, and many little islands appear. We passed in and out among these islands for about three miles, when the river contracted to its usual width, but islands and bars were common all the way, and the current is about five miles an hour.

After passing a long bank called Hoochecoo Bluff, the river again spreads out into a very archipelago. For three or four miles it is nearly a mile from bank to bank, but so close and numerous are the little islands that it is often difficult to tell where the shores of the river are.

At the confluence of the Pelly and the Lewis the country is low, with extensive terraced flats, running back to rounded hills and ridges. The Pelly is about two hundred yards wide at its mouth, and from there these great waters flow swiftly on in an uninterrupted course one thousand six hundred and fifty miles to the Bering Sea. The Yukon, below the junction, averages about a quarter of a mile wide, with a current which carries everything swiftly along. It is dotted by many little islands, and we quickly came to the ruins of old Fort Selkirk, a trading post which was established by the Hudson Bay Company in 1848. Indians pillaged and set fire to it in 1853, leaving nothing but the remains of two chimneys, which are still standing. The place has been put to some later uses, however, an English church mission and an Indian village being established there, and for some time Arthur Harper, whom we have already mentioned as a pioneer in these regions, maintained a trading post there. Here we were enabled to use some of the money we had brought along in case of emergency, and which we had saved by packing our goods, in the purchase of new supplies, but it did not enable us to put in all we could wish, for goods are high after they have been brought up the long Yukon. But we were glad to have a tent again, and some articles which are a prime necessity in such a country. It felt as if we had again come in touch with civilization.

We had made good time from the lakes and were in good health, but it had been a long, hard voyage and it always will be, in any time of the year, till modern methods of communication have overcome some of the terrible obstacles. All along the route we had noted the graves of those who have been lost in previous years on this route. Both Indians and white men have fallen in the struggle to press into the great valley of the Yukon by the Dyea trail. And we heard of others, beside the two drowned in the cañon, who lost their lives that same spring in which we came in. One man was killed in the Five Finger Rapids, but Joe and I were safe at last on the waters of the mighty river, and he who will never stop to think of an overruling Providence in the feverish rush of life in the busy centers of the United States, must in these immense regions, where he feels so small, where he finds so little to measure himself by, feel a sense of gratitude filling his whole being as he stands strong and unhurt at the end of such a voyage.

The Creeks

The creeks of the Klondike region were described as being elaborately abundant. Stories outside the Yukon were of gold fields so rich you simply had to bend over and pick up nuggets. And while this was true for some of the richest claims at the start of the gold rush most people had to toil to get their gold.

The lone prospector swishing gold in a pan is the way the gold rush was described in the south. Initially, panning was the predominant means of extracting gold from the sands of the various creeks of the Klondike valley. With time, sluices and rocker boxes were constructed to sift the gravel more efficiently. The only limitation was one's ability to access enough gravel because most of the year the ground is frozen solid.

Many searched for gold by going underground. Claustrophobic tunnels crisscrossed as stampeders searched for a "pay streak." Tunneling in the north is difficult because of the permafrost, a layer of earth, which remains frozen throughout the year. Thawing this layer was done by setting large underground wood fires and then winching bucket after bucket of singed earth out of the mine. Once beyond the layer of permafrost, miners used pickaxe, shovel and bare hands to excavate. Candles flickered in the damp, narrow passageways. Most mines were more than thirty feet below the surface, and few went deeper than a hundred feet.

Day laborers could make as much as $15 a day, and many received bonuses and other incentives to work as quickly as possible. They would never get rich, although day laborers often did very well working these claims.

To Build a Fire
Jack London

Day had broken cold and gray, exceeding cold and gray, when the man turned aside from the main Yukon trail and climbed the high earth bank, where a dim and little traveled trail led eastward through fat spruce timberland. It was a steep bank, and he paused for breath at the top, excusing the act to himself by looking at his watch. It was nine o'clock. There was no sun nor hint of sun, though there was not a cloud in the sky. It was a clear day, and yet there seemed an intangible pall over the face of things, a subtle gloom that made the day dark, and that was due to the absence of sun. This fact did not worry the man. He was used to the lack of sun. It had been days since he had seen the sun, and he knew that a few more days must pass before that cheerful orb, due south, would just peep above the sky-line and dip immediately from view.

The man flung a look back along the way he had come. The Yukon lay a mile wide and hidden under three feet of ice. On top of this ice were as many feet of snow. It was all pure white, rolling in gentle undulations where the ice-jams of the freeze-up had formed. North and south, as far as his eye could see, it was unbroken white, save for a dark hair-line that curved and twisted from around the spruce-covered island to the south, and that curved and twisted away into the north, where it disappeared behind another spruce-covered island. This dark hairline was the trail — the main trail — that led south five hundred miles to the Chilkoot Pass, Dyea, and salt water; and that led north seventy miles to Dawson, and still on to the north a thousand miles to Nulato, and finally to St. Michael on Bering Sea, a thousand miles and half a thousand more.

But all this — the mysterious, far-reaching hair-line trail, the absence of sun from the sky, the tremendous cold, and the strangeness and weirdness of it all — made no impression on the man. It was not because he was long used to it. He was a newcomer in the land, a *chechaquo*, and this was his first winter. The trouble with him was that he was without imagination. He was quick and alert in the things of life, but only in the things, and not in the significances. Fifty degrees below zero meant eighty-odd degrees of frost. Such fact impressed him as being cold and uncomfortable, and that was all. It did not lead him to meditate upon his frailty as a creature of temperature, and upon man's frailty in general, able only to live within certain narrow limits of heat and cold; and from there on it did not lead him to the conjectural field of immortality and man's place in the universe. Fifty degrees below zero stood for a bite of frost that hurt and that must be guarded against by the use of mittens, earflaps, warm moccasins, and thick socks. Fifty degrees below zero was to him just precisely fifty degrees below zero. That there should be anything more to it than that was a thought that never entered his head.

As he turned to go on, he spat speculatively. There was a sharp, explosive crackle that startled him. He spat again. And again, in the air, before it could fall to the snow, the spittle crackled. He knew that at fifty below spittle crackled on the snow, but this spittle had crackled in the air. Undoubtedly it was colder than fifty below — how much colder he did not know. But the temperature did not matter. He was bound for the old claim on the left fork of Henderson Creek, where the boys were already. They had come over across the divide from the Indian Creek country, while he had come the roundabout way to take a look at the possibilities of getting out logs in the spring from the islands in the Yukon. He would be in to camp by six o'clock; a bit after dark, it was true, but the boys would be there, a fire would be going, and a hot supper would be ready. As for lunch, he pressed his hand against the protruding bundle under his jacket. It was also under his shirt, wrapped up in a handkerchief and lying against the naked skin. It was the only way to keep the biscuits from freezing. He smiled agreeably to himself as he thought of those biscuits, each cut open and sopped in bacon grease, and each enclosing a generous slice of fried bacon.

He plunged in among the big spruce trees. The trail was faint. A foot of snow had fallen since the last sled had passed over, and he was glad he was without a sled, traveling light. In fact, he carried nothing but the lunch wrapped in the handkerchief. He was surprised, however, at the cold. It certainly was cold, he concluded, as he rubbed his numb nose and cheekbones with his mittened hand. He was a warm-whiskered man, but the hair on his face did not protect the high cheekbones and the eager nose that thrust itself aggressively into the frosty air.

At the man's heels trotted a dog, a big native husky, the proper wolf dog, gray-coated and without any visible or temperamental difference from its brother, the wild wolf. The animal was depressed by the tremendous cold. It knew that it was no time for traveling. Its instinct told it a truer tale than was told to the man by the man's judgment. In reality, it was not merely colder than fifty below zero; it was colder than sixty below, than seventy below. It was seventy-five below zero. Since the freezing point is thirty-two above zero, it meant that one hundred and seven degrees of frost obtained. The dog did not know anything about thermometers. Possibly in its brain there was no sharp consciousness of a condition of very cold such as was in the man's brain. But the brute had its instinct. It experienced a vague but menacing apprehension that subdued it and made it slink along at the man's heels, and that made it question eagerly every unwonted movement of the man as if expecting him to go into camp or to seek shelter somewhere and build a fire. The dog had learned fire, and it wanted fire, or else to burrow under the snow and cuddle its warmth away from the air.

The frozen moisture of its breathing had settled on its fur in a fine powder of frost, and especially were its jowls, muzzle, and eyelashes whitened by its crystalled breath. The man's red beard and mustache were likewise frosted, but more solidly, the deposit taking the form of ice and increasing with every warm, moist breath he exhaled. Also, the man was chewing tobacco, and the muzzle of ice held his lips so rigidly that he was unable to clear his chin when he expelled the juice. The result was that a crystal beard of the color and solidity of amber was increasing its length on his chin. If he fell down it would shatter itself, like glass, into brittle fragments. But he did not mind the appendage. It was the penalty all tobacco-chewers paid in that country and he had been out before in two cold snaps. They had not been so cold as this, he knew, not by the spirit thermometer at Sixty Mile. He knew they had been registered at fifty below and at fifty-five.

He held on through the level stretch of woods for several miles, crossed a wide flat of niggerheads, and dropped down a bank to the frozen bed of a small stream. This was Henderson Creek, and he knew he was ten miles from the forks. He looked at his watch. It was ten o'clock. He was making four miles an hour, and he calculated that he would arrive at the forks at half-past twelve. He decided to celebrate that event by eating his lunch there.

The dog dropped in again at his heels, with a tail drooping discouragement, as the man swung along the creek-bed. The furrow of the old sled-trail was plainly visible, but a dozen inches of snow covered the marks of the last runners. In a month no man had come up or down that silent creek. The man held steadily on. He was not much given to thinking, and just then particularly he had nothing to think about save that he would eat lunch at the forks and that at six o'clock he would be in camp with the boys. There was nobody to talk to; and, had there been, speech would have been impossible because of the ice-muzzle on his mouth. So he continued monotonously to chew tobacco and to increase the length of his amber beard.

Once in a while the thought reiterated itself that it was very cold and that he had never experienced such cold. As he walked along he rubbed his cheekbones and nose with the back of his mittened hand. He did this automatically, now and again changing hands. But rub as he would, the instant he stopped his cheekbones went numb, and the following instant the end of his nose went numb. He was sure to frost his cheeks; he knew that, and experienced a pang of regret that he had not devised a nose-strap of the sort Bud wore in cold snaps. Such a strap passed across the cheeks, as well, and saved them. But it didn't matter much, after all. What were frosted cheeks? A bit painful, that was all; they were never serious.

Empty as the man's mind was of thoughts, he was keenly observant, and he noticed the changes in the creek, the curves and bends and timber — jams, and always he sharply noted where he placed his feet. Once, coming around a bend, he shied abruptly, like a startled horse curved away from the place where he had been walking, and retreated several paces back along the trail. The creek he knew was frozen clear to the bottom, — no creek could contain water in that arctic winter, — but he knew also that there were springs that bubbled out from the hillsides and ran along under the snow and on top of the ice of the creek. He knew that the coldest snaps never froze these springs, and he knew likewise their danger. They were traps. They hid pools of water under the snow that might be three inches deep, or three feet. Sometimes a skin of ice half an inch thick covered them, and in turn was covered by the snow. Sometimes there were alternate layers of water and ice skin, so that when one broke through he kept on breaking through for a while, sometimes wetting himself to the waist.

That was why he had shied in such panic. He had felt the give under his feet and heard the crackle of a snow-hidden ice-skin. And to get his feet wet in such a temperature meant trouble and danger. At the very least it meant delay, for he would be forced to stop and build a fire, and under its protection to bare his feet while he dried his socks and moccasins. He stood and studied the creek-bed and its banks, and decided that the flow of water came from the right. He reflected awhile, rubbing his nose and cheeks, then skirted to the left, stepping gingerly and testing the footing for each step. Once clear of the danger, he took a fresh chew of tobacco and swung along at his four-mile gait.

In the course of the next two hours he came upon several similar traps. Usually the snow above the hidden pools had a sunken, candied appearance that advertised the danger. Once again, however, he had a close call; and once, suspecting danger, he compelled the dog to go on in front. The dog did not want to go. It hung back until the man shoved it forward, and then it went quickly across the white, unbroken surface. Suddenly it broke through, floundered to one side, and got away to firmer footing. It had wet its forefeet and legs, and almost immediately the water that clung to it turned to ice. It made quick efforts to lick the ice off its legs, then dropped down in the snow and began to bite out the ice that had formed between the toes. This was a matter of instinct. To permit the ice to remain would mean sore feet. It did not know this. It merely obeyed the mysterious prompting that arose from the deep crypts of its being. But the man knew, having achieved a judgment on the subject, and he removed the mitten from his right hand and helped tear out the ice-particles. He did not expose his fingers more than a minute, and was astonished at the swift numbness that smote them. It certainly was cold. He pulled on the mitten hastily, and beat the hand savagely across his chest.

At twelve o'clock the day was at its brightest. Yet the sun was too far south on its winter journey to clear the horizon. The bulge of the earth intervened between it and Henderson Creek, where the man walked under a clear sky at noon and cast no shadow. At half past twelve, to the minute, he arrived at the forks of the creek. He was pleased at the speed he had made. If he kept it up, he would certainly be with the boys by six. He unbuttoned his jacket and shirt and drew forth his lunch. The action consumed no more than a quarter of a minute, yet in that brief moment the numbness laid hold of the exposed fingers. He did not put the mitten on, but, instead, struck the fingers a dozen sharp smashes against his leg. Then he sat down on a snow-covered log to eat. The sting that followed upon the striking of his fingers against his leg ceased so quickly that he was startled. He had had no chance to take a bite of biscuit. He struck the fingers repeatedly and returned them to the mitten, baring the other hand for the purpose of eating. He tried to take a mouthful, but the ice-muzzle prevented. He had forgotten to build a fire and thaw out. He chuckled at his foolishness, and as he chuckled he noted the numbness creeping into the exposed fingers. Also, he noted that the stinging which had first come to his toes when he sat down was already passing away. He wondered whether the toes were warm or numb. He moved them inside the moccasins and decided that they were numb.

He pulled the mitten on hurriedly and stood up. He was a bit frightened. He stamped up and down until the stinging returned into the feet. It certainly was cold, was his thought. That man from Sulphur Creek had spoken the truth when telling how cold it sometimes got in the country. And he had laughed at him at the time! That showed one must not be too sure of things. There was no mistake about it, it was cold. He strode up and down, stamping his feet and threshing his arms, until reassured by the returning warmth. Then he got out matches and proceeded to make a fire. From the undergrowth, where the high water of the previous spring had lodged a supply of seasoned twigs, he got his firewood. Working carefully from a small beginning, he soon had a roaring fire, over which he thawed the ice from his face and in the protection of which he ate his biscuits. For the moment the cold of space was outwitted. The dog took satisfaction in the fire, stretching out close enough for warmth and far enough away to escape being singed.

When the man had finished, he filled his pipe and took his comfortable time over a smoke. Then he pulled on his mittens, settled the earflaps of his cap firmly about his ears, and took the creek trail up the left fork. The dog was disappointed and yearned back toward the fire. This man did not know cold. Possibly all the generations of his ancestry had been ignorant of cold, of real cold, of cold one hundred and seven degrees below freezing point. But the dog knew; all its ancestry knew, and it had inherited the knowledge. And it knew that it was not good to walk abroad in such fearful cold. It was the time to lie snug in a hole in the snow and wait for a curtain of cloud to be drawn across the face of outer space whence this cold came. On the other hand, there was no keen intimacy between the dog and the man. The one was the toil slave of the other, and the only caresses it had ever received were the caresses of the whiplash and of harsh and menacing throat-sounds that threatened the whiplash. So the dog made no effort to communicate its apprehension to the man. It was not concerned in the welfare of the man; it was for its own sake that it yearned back toward the fire. But the man whistled, and spoke to it with the sound of whiplashes, and the dog swung in at the man's heels and followed after.

The man took a chew of tobacco and proceeded to start a new amber beard. Also, his moist breath quickly powdered with white his mustache, eyebrows, and lashes. There did not seem to be so many springs on the left fork of the Henderson, and for half an hour the man saw no signs of any. And then it happened. At a place where there were no signs, where the soft, unbroken snow seemed to advertise solidity beneath, the man broke through. It was not deep. He wet himself halfway to the knees before he floundered out to the firm crust.

He was angry, and cursed his luck aloud. He had hoped to get into camp with the boys at six o'clock, and this would delay him an hour, for he would have to build a fire and dry out his footgear. This was imperative at that low temperature — he knew that much; and he turned aside to the bank, which he climbed. On top, tangled in the underbrush about the trunks of several small spruce trees, was a high-water deposit of dry fire-wood-sticks and twigs, principally, but also larger portions of seasoned branches and fine, dry, last-year's grasses. He threw down several large pieces on top of the snow. This served for a foundation and prevented the young flame from drowning itself in the snow it otherwise would melt. The flame he got by touching a match to a small shred of birch-bark that he took from his pocket. This burned even more readily than paper. Placing it on the foundation, he fed the young flame with wisps of dry grass and with the tiniest dry twigs.

He worked slowly and carefully, keenly aware of his danger. Gradually, as the flame grew stronger, he increased the size of the twigs which he fed it. He squatted in the snow, pulling the twigs from their entanglement in the brush and feeding them directly to the flame. He knew there must be no failure. When it is seventy-five below zero, a man must not fail in his first attempt to build a fire — that is, if his feet are wet. If his feet are dry, and he fails, he can run along the trail for half a mile and restore his circulation. But the circulation of wet and freezing feet cannot be restored by running when it is seventy-five below. No matter how fast he runs, the wet feet will freeze harder.

All this the man knew. The old-timer on Sulphur Creek had told him about it the previous fall, and now he was appreciating the advice. Already all sensation had gone out of his feet. To build the fire he had been forced to remove his mittens, and the fingers had quickly gone numb. His pace of four miles an hour had kept his heart pumping blood to the surface of his body and to all the extremities. But the instant he stopped, the action of the pump eased down. The cold of space smote the unprotected tip of the planet, and he, being on that unprotected tip, received the full force of the blow. The blood of his body recoiled before it. The blood was alive, like the dog, and like the dog it wanted to hide away and cover itself up from the fearful cold. So long as he walked four miles an hour, he pumped that blood willy-nilly to the surface; but now it ebbed away and sank down into the recesses of his body. The extremities were the first to feel its absence. His wet feet froze the faster, and his exposed fingers numbed the faster, though they had not yet begun to freeze. Nose and cheeks were already freezing, while the skin of all his body chilled as it lost its own blood.

But he was safe. Toes and nose and cheeks would be only touched by the frost, for the fire was beginning to burn with strength. He was feeding it with twigs the size of his finger. In another minute he would be able to feed it with branches the size of his wrist, and then he could remove his wet footgear, and, while it dried, he could keep his naked feet warm by the fire, rubbing them at first, of course, with snow. The fire was a success. He was safe. He remembered the advice of the old-timer on Sulphur Creek and smiled. The old-timer had been very serious in laying down the law that no man must travel alone in the Klondike after fifty below. Well, here he was; he had had the accident; he was alone; and he had saved himself. Those old-timers were rather womanish, some of them, he thought. All a man had to do was to keep his head, and he was all right. Any man who was a man could travel alone. But it was surprising the rapidity with which his cheeks and nose were freezing. And he had not thought his fingers could go lifeless in so short a time. Lifeless they were, for he could scarcely make them move together to grip a twig, and they seemed remote from his body and from him. When he touched a twig, he had to look and see whether or not he had hold of it. The wires were pretty well down between him and his finger-ends.

All of which counted for little. There was the fire, snapping and crackling and promising life with every dancing flame. He started to untie his moccasins. They were coated with ice; the thick German socks were like sheaths of iron halfway to the knees; and the moccasin strings were like rods of steel all twisted and knotted as by some conflagration. For a moment he tugged with his numb fingers then, realizing the folly of it, he drew his sheath knife.

But before he could cut the strings it happened. It was his own fault, or rather, his mistake. He should not have built the fire under the spruce tree. He should have built it in the open. But it had been easier to pull the twigs from the brush and drop them directly on the fire. Now the tree under which he had done this carried weight of snow on its boughs. No wind had blown for weeks, and each bough was fully freighted. Each time he had pulled a twig he had communicated a slight agitation to the tree — an imperceptible agitation, so far as he was concerned, but an agitation sufficient to bring about the disaster. High up in the tree one bough capsized its load of snow. This fell on the boughs beneath, capsizing them. This process continued spreading out and involving the whole tree. It grew like an avalanche, and it descended without warning upon the man and the fire, and the fire was blotted out. Where it had burned was a mantle of fresh and disordered snow.

The man was shocked. It was as though he had just heard his own sentence of death. For a moment he sat and stared at the spot where the fire had been. Then he grew very calm. Perhaps the old-timer on Sulphur Creek was right. If he had only had a trail-mate he would have been in no danger now. The trail-mate could have built the fire. Well, it was up to him to build the fire over again, and this second time there must be no failure. Even if he succeeded, he would most likely lose some toes. His feet must be badly frozen by now, and there would be some time before the second fire was ready.

Such were his thoughts, but he did not sit and think them. He was busy all the time they were passing through his mind. He made a new foundation for a fire, this time in the open, where no treacherous tree could blot it out. Next, he gathered dry grasses and tiny twigs from the high-water flotsam. He could not bring his fingers together to pull them out, but he was able to gather them by the handful. In this way he got many rotten twigs and bits of green moss that were undesirable, but it was the best he could do. He worked methodically, even collecting an armful of the larger branches to be used later when the fire gathered strength. And all the while the dog sat and watched him, a certain yearning wistfulness in its eyes, for it looked upon him as the fire-provider, and the fire was slow in coming.

When all was ready, the man reached in his pocket for a second piece of birch-bark. He knew the bark was there, and, though he could not feel it with his fingers, he could hear its crisp rustling as he fumbled for it. Try as he would, he could not clutch hold of it. And all the time, in his consciousness, was the knowledge that each instant his feet were freezing. This thought tended to put him in a panic, but he fought against it and kept calm. He pulled on his mittens with his teeth, and threshed his arms back and forth, beating his hands with all his might against his sides. He did this sitting down, and he stood up to do it; and all the while the dog sat in the snow, its wolf-brush of a tail curled around warmly over its forefeet, its sharp wolf-ears pricked forward intently as it watched the man. And the man, as he beat and threshed with his arms and hands, felt a great surge of envy as he regarded the creature that was warm and secure in its natural covering.

After a time he was aware of the first far-away signals of sensation in his beaten fingers. The faint tingling grew stronger till it evolved into a stinging ache that was excruciating, but which the man hailed with satisfaction. He stripped the mitten from his right hand and fetched forth the birch-bark. The exposed fingers were quickly going numb again. Next he brought out his bunch of sulphur matches. But the tremendous cold had already driven the life out of his fingers. In his effort to separate one match from the others, the whole bunch fell in the snow. He tried to pick it out of the snow, but failed. The dead fingers could neither touch nor clutch. He was very careful. He drove the thought of his freezing feet, and nose, and cheeks, out of his mind, devoting his whole soul to the matches. He watched, using the sense of vision in place of that of touch, and when he saw his fingers on each side the bunch, he closed them — that is, he willed to close them, for the wires were down, and the fingers did not obey. He pulled the mitten on the right hand, and beat it fiercely against his knee. Then, with both mittened hands, he scooped the bunch of matches, along with much snow, into his lap. Yet he was no better off.

After some manipulation he managed to get the bunch between the heels of his mittened hands. In this fashion he carried it to his mouth. The ice crackled and snapped when by a violent effort he opened his mouth. He drew the lower jaw in, curled the upper lip out of the way, and scraped the bunch with his upper teeth in order to separate a match. He succeeded in getting one, which he dropped on his lap. He was no better off. He could not pick it up. Then he devised a way. He picked it up in his teeth and scratched it on his leg. Twenty times he scratched before he succeeded in lighting it. As it flamed he held it with his teeth to the birch-bark. But the burning brimstone went up his nostrils and into his lungs, causing him to cough spasmodically. The match fell into the snow and went out.

The old-timer on Sulphur Creek was right, he thought in the moment of controlled despair that ensued: after fifty below, a man should travel with a partner. He beat his hands, but failed in exciting any sensation. Suddenly he bared both hands, removing the mittens with his teeth. He caught the whole bunch between the heels of his hands. His arm muscles not being frozen enabled him to press the hand-heels tightly against the matches. Then he scratched the bunch along his leg. It flared into flame, seventy sulphur matches at once! There was no wind to blow them out. He kept his head to one side to escape the strangling fumes, and held the blasting bunch to the birch bark. As he so held it, he became aware of sensation in his hand. His flesh was burning. He could smell it. Deep down below the surface he could feel it. The sensation developed into pain that grew acute. And still he endured it holding the flame of the matches clumsily to the bark that would not light readily because his own burning hands were in the way, absorbing most of the flame.

At last, when he could endure no more, he jerked his hands apart. The blazing matches fell sizzling into the snow, but the birch bark was alight. He began laying dry grasses and the tiniest twigs on the flame. He could not pick and choose, for he had to lift the fuel between the heels of his hands. Small pieces of rotten wood and green moss clung to the twigs and he bit them off as well as he could with his teeth. He cherished the flame carefully and awkwardly. It meant life, and it must not perish. The withdrawal of blood from the surface of his body now made him begin to shiver, and he grew more awkward. A large piece of green moss fell squarely on the little fire. He tried to poke it out with his fingers, but his shivering frame made him poke too far, and he disrupted the nucleus of the little fire, the hurtling grasses and tiny twigs separating and scattering. He tried to poke them together again, but in spite of the tenseness of the effort, his shivering got away with him, and the twigs were hopelessly scattered. Each twig gushed a puff of smoke and went out. The fire-provider had failed. As he looked apathetically about him, his eyes chanced on the dog, sitting across the ruins of the fire from him, in the snow, making restless, hunching movements, slightly lifting one forefoot and then the other, shifting its weight back and forth on them with wistful eagerness.

The sight of the dog put a wild idea into his head. He remembered the tale of the man, caught in a blizzard, who killed a steer and crawled inside the carcass, and so was saved. He would kill the dog and bury his hands in the warm body until the numbness went out of them. Then he could build another fire He spoke to the dog, calling it to him; but in his voice was a strange note of fear that frightened the animal, who had never known the man to speak in such way before. Something was the matter, and its suspicious nature sensed danger — it knew not what danger, but somewhere, somehow, in its brain arose an apprehension of the man. It flattened its ears down at the sound of the man's voice, and its restless, bunching movements and the liftings and shiftings of its forefeet became more pronounced; but it would not come to the man. He got on his hands and knees and crawled toward the dog. This unusual posture again excited suspicion, and the animal sidled mincingly away.

The man sat up in the snow for a moment and struggled for calmness. Then he pulled on his mittens, by means of his teeth, and got up on his feet. He glanced down at first in order to assure himself that he was really standing up, for the absence of sensation in his feet left him unrelated to the earth. His erect position in itself started to drive the webs of suspicion from the dog's mind; and when he spoke peremptorily, with the sound of whiplashes in his voice, the dog rendered its customary allegiance and came to him. As it came within reaching distance, the man lost his control. His arms flashed out to the dog, and he experienced genuine surprise when he discovered that his hands could not clutch, that there was neither bend nor feeling in the fingers. He had forgotten for the moment that they were frozen and that they were freezing more and more. All this happened quickly and before the animal could get away, he encircled its body with his arms. He sat down in the snow, and in this fashion held the dog, while it snarled and whined and struggled.

But it was all he could do, to hold his body encircled in his arms and sit there. He realized he could not kill the dog. There was no way to do it. With his helpless hands he could neither draw nor hold his sheath knife nor throttle the animal. He released it, and it plunged away, with tail between its legs, and still snarling. It halted forty feet away and surveyed him curiously, with ears sharply pricked forward. The man looked down at his hands in order to locate them, and found them hanging at the end of his arms. It struck him as curious that one should have to use his eyes in order to find out where his hands were. He began threshing his arms back and forth, beating the mittened hands against his sides. He did this for five minutes, violently, and his heart pumped enough blood up to the surface to put a stop to his shivering. But no sensation aroused in his hands. He had an impression that they hung like weights on the end of his arms, but when he tried to run the impression down, he could not find it.

A certain fear of death, dull and oppressive came to him. This fear quickly became poignant as he realized that it was no longer a mere matter of freezing his fingers and toes, or of losing his hands and feet, but that it was a matter of life and death with the chances against him. This threw him into a panic, and he turned and ran up the creek-bed along the old, dim trail. The dog joined in behind and kept up with him. He ran blindly, without intention, in fear such as he had never known in his life. Slowly, as he ploughed and floundered through the snow, he began to see things again, — the banks of the creek, the old timber-jams, the leafless aspens, and the sky. The running made him feel better. He did not shiver. Maybe, if he ran on, his feet would thaw out; and, anyway, if he ran far enough, he would reach camp and the boys. Without doubt he would lose some fingers and toes and some of his face; but the boys would take care of him, and save the rest of him when he got there. And at the same time there was another thought in his mind that said he would never get to the camp and the boys; that it was too many miles away, that the freezing had too great a start on him and that he would soon be stiff and dead.

This thought he kept in the background and refused to consider. Sometimes it pushed itself forward and demanded to be heard, but he thrust it back and strove to think of other things.

It struck him as curious that he could run at all on feet so frozen that he could not feel them when they struck the earth and took the weight of his body. He seemed to himself to skim along above the surface, and to have no connection with the earth. Somewhere he had once seen a winged Mercury, and he wondered if Mercury felt as he felt when skimming over the earth.

His theory of running until he reached camp and the boys had one flaw in it: he lacked the endurance. Several times he stumbled, and finally he tottered, crumpled up, and fell. When he tried to rise, he failed. He must sit and rest, he decided, and next time he would merely walk and keep on going. As he sat and regained his breath, he noted that he was feeling quite warm and comfortable. He was not shivering, and it even seemed that a warm glow had come to his chest and trunk. And yet, when he touched his nose or cheeks, there was no sensation. Running would not thaw them out. Nor would it thaw out his hands and feet. Then the thought came to him that the frozen portions of his body must be extending. He tried to keep this thought down, to forget it, to think of something else; he was aware of the panicky feeling that it caused, and he was afraid of the panic. But the thought asserted itself, and persisted, until it produced a vision of his body totally frozen. This was too much, and he made another wild run along the trail. Once he slowed down to a walk, but the thought of the freezing extending itself made him run again.

And all the time the dog ran with him at his heels. When he fell down a second time, it curled its tail over its forefeet and sat in front of him, facing him, curiously eager and intent. The warmth and security of the animal angered him, and he cursed it till it flattened down its ears appeasingly. This time the shivering came more quickly upon the man. He was losing in his battle with the frost. It was creeping into his body from all sides. The thought of it drove him on, but he ran no more than a hundred feet, when he staggered and pitched headlong. It was his last panic. When he had recovered his breath and control, he sat up and entertained in his mind the conception of meeting death with dignity. However, the conception did not come to him in such terms. His idea of it was that he had been making a fool of himself, running around like a chicken with its head cut off — such was the simile that occurred to him. Well, he was bound to freeze anyway, and he might as well take it decently. With this newfound peace of mind came the first glimmer of drowsiness. A good idea, he thought, to sleep off to death. It was like taking an anaesthetic. Freezing was not so bad as people thought. There were lots of worse ways to die.

He pictured the boys finding his body the next day. Suddenly he found himself with them, coming along the trail and looking for himself. And, still with them, he came around a turn in the trail and found himself lying in the snow. He did not belong with himself anymore, for even then he was out of himself, standing with the boys and looking at himself in the snow. It certainly was cold, was his thought. When he got back to the States he could tell the folks what real cold was. He drifted on from this to a vision of the old-timer on Sulphur Creek. He could see him quite clearly, warm and comfortable, and smoking a pipe.

"You were right, old hoss; you were right," the man mumbled to the old-timer on Sulphur Creek.

Then the man drowsed off into what seemed to him the most comfortable and satisfying sleep he had ever known. The dog sat facing him and waiting. The brief day drew to a close in a long, slow twilight. There were no signs of a fire to be made, and, besides, never in the dog's experience had it known a man to sit like that in the snow and make no fire. As the twilight grew on, its eager yearning for the fire mastered it, and with a great lifting and shifting of its forefeet, it whined softly, then flattened its ears down in anticipation of being chidden by the man. But the man remained silent. Later, the dog whined loudly. And still later it crept close to the man and caught the scent of death. This made the animal bristle and back away. A little longer it delayed, howling under the stars that leaped and danced and shone brightly in the cold sky. Then it turned and trotted up the trail in the direction of the camp it knew, where the other food providers and fire providers were.

Methods of Mining
William Ogilvie

I will now describe the methods of mining in vogue in the early days, and compare them with those of more recent date. We have already seen that the first mining done in the territory was confined to the bars and banks of the streams, for the reason that it was considered impossible to reach bedrock as in other regions, where less frost prevailed. In those days the principal means of separating the fine gold from the sand and gravel was the rocker. In all the methods used a common principle existed; that is, the principle of gravity. Gold is nineteen times heavier than water, and seven to eight times heavier than rock, and although native gold is never pure, consequently lighter than pure, the difference does not affect the principle of extraction. Generally, then, the practical application of the principle to the separation of the precious metal from the dirt holding it, is an inclined plane, over which a stream of water is made to flow.

The gold-bearing dirt is shoveled into the fast-flowing stream, which carries along the lighter material and leaves the heavy gold behind. To aid in arresting and holding the gold, barriers are put in the bottom of the trough where there is plenty of water, and a head can be had, that is, if the water can be taken from a higher level to a lower one, a series of troughs are made of plank, as wide as possible consistent with the supply of water. These are elevated on trestles or other appliances, so that the water enters the high end and flows through them. They are fitted into each other at the joints, so that the stream is continuous, and the line of three or more "sluice boxes," as they are termed, is sloped, to give the water momentum enough to carry down the gravel and sand, yet hardly move the gold. The progress of the metal is finally stopped by the barriers, called "riffles." These are in up-to-date gold-saving plants made of angle iron, cut into lengths the width of the sluice box, and bolted together at a constant distance from each other, in groups resembling a large gridiron. The groups are, of course, limited in size for convenience in handling.

Sometimes, especially when the gold is fine, expanded metal and coco-matting are associated with the riffles. The metal is laid on top of the matting, so that its bars throw down the fine material and the gold is entrapped in the matting. The bars of angle iron in the riffles are set about an inch apart. The spaces soon fill with sand and fine gravel, but the small cataract formed by the water falling over each bar keeps a basin between them in which the gold and heavy material remains, the heavier bits at the top, and the lighter scattered along in proportion to their size and weight; and the very lightest in the coco-matting. In the early days the riffles were made of bars of wood, generally sections of small trees, cut in convenient lengths, placed parallel to each other, and held in that position by a section of plank nailed to their ends. These sections of riffles, unlike those made of angle iron, were placed longitudinally with the sluice box, instead of transversely. That system is all right where the gold is very coarse, but with fine gold a lot of it escapes. Small stones soon got wedged between the wooden bars, and pits in the sand were formed between them, as in the case of the angle-iron bars.

Variations of the sluice box and riffles constitute all the methods of washing gold. Where the sluice box could be used, it always was, but it is obvious that on bar and bank mining there would be but few places where the miner could avail himself of it, and those only where a stream joining the main one came in with a rapid descent. Generally the fall in the box had to be about one in four or five to get the best results, so that in thirty feet of box there had to be a head, or drop, of five to seven feet. The sluice box enabled the operator to work a great deal more dirt than by any other system of manual labor. The material was simply thrown into the head of the line of boxes, the water did the rest. Bringing the dirt to the box was the greatest part of the labor.

Where the sluice box could not be utilized for lack of a head of water the rocker had to be employed. As its name implies, it is a box some three or four feet in length, and twenty to twenty-four inches wide, placed on a pair of rockers, such as might be found on an old-fashioned household cradle. On top of this box a shallow box or hopper with a thin iron-plate bottom was placed. The iron plate was plentifully punched with quarter-inch holes. Below this cover was one or more sloping shelves, covered with a bit of blanket or, in some cases, a small riffle. Close beside a stream or pool of water, two hewed blocks were firmly fixed in the ground, and on these the rockers of the machine were placed.

The operator took his place beside the rocker with a long handled dipper in one hand, and the other ready to rock. If alone, he first filled the shallow box with fine gravel, rejecting all the coarse parts. He then ladled water on to the mass, at the same time rocking the machine from side to side; the water and motion combined carried the finer and heavier parts of the sand and gravel through the holes in the iron plate, and they fell on to the inclined shelves below down which they were sluiced by the water, the gold being caught by the wool of the blanket or in the riffles, as the case might be. If two or more persons were working in partnership, one carried gravel and loaded the hopper, while the other rocked. Several times a day the blankets or riffles were taken out and washed in a tub of water to get the gold out of them. They were then replaced and the work resumed. This process, it is evident, is slow and laborious, but there were many places where it was the only method available. By it a pair of men could clean from one and a half to four cubic yards per day. With sluice boxes and a plentiful supply of water, many times that quantity could be washed.

When we reflect that two men by this method averaged about one hundred dollars per day on the bars of Stewart River, we can form some idea of the richness of the ground they worked. When we are told that six men during a little more than two months took out by this tedious, laborious process about thirty-five thousand dollars from one of the famous bars of that stream, it surprises us. But when we recollect that at many other places along the banks and bars of the Yukon and Hootalinqua men were making very good wages by this process when the discovery of coarse gold on Forty-Mile put a period to bar and bank diggings, we can form some estimate of the future of the region when dredge and other approved methods of mining such ground, under the conditions existing there, are installed on the scale the region justifies.

As we have seen, firing the bars in the early spring months during the period of the very lowest water, to get the richer parts of the deposits, which were inaccessible in summer, led to firing or thawing to bedrock. This gave a tremendous advance to mining in this hitherto "skim" mining region, as it was considered. It opened regions of ground before thought impossible, and made room for scores where one had been considered enough.

Vast improvement as it was, it was very expensive and wasteful of fuel. The fire was not confined — it could not be — to produce the best result. Naturally ascending, the heat thawed a great deal more ground than held pay, and this had to be handled with the rest, greatly reducing the average per yard of the dirt worked, and at the same time increasing the cost of working in the same ratio. The pay streak was often not more than three feet in depth, and the burning thawed seven, eight, and nine feet. During the winter of 1897 much discussion was held by the miners concerning the improvement of the firing method. All sorts of ways were proposed, only to be dropped after thorough examination; but two stood out prominently and permanently, namely, thawing by steam, and thawing by coal oil or gasoline flames.

The latter idea was an enlarged plumber's torch, the intense flame of which was to be directed against the wall of frozen earth. Of the two, the steam was considered the most adequate, but the gasoline torch was more portable, involving no boiler or wood; the cost of the gasoline, however, at that time — and yet — one dollar per gallon, was prohibitive, no matter what the practical merit of the method might prove; and though wood became more and more scarce, it never got high enough in cost to reach the level of the gasoline. The gasoline torch was tried, but its action was too slow and too local. Steam at a pressure of about forty pounds to the inch was carried in flexible hose, and applied through "points," that is, a section of half-inch iron pipe five or six feet long, into one end of which a steel plug is inserted. In this are bored two or three holes one-eighth of an inch in diameter, through which the steam issues against the frozen gravel, and thaws it at an astonishing rate. The points were held against the wall till driven into it their full length, and were then left to do their work. This process did a great deal more work with the same amount of wood, and, better still, the limits of the work were much more under control. With improved hoisting machinery, better sluice boxes and riffles, ground could be worked with good profit that would not be touched in the earlier years of the territory.

Dredging was first thought of as a mode of developing some of the ground in the winter of 1898. While I was in London a syndicate which owned a valuable piece of ground in the Klondike consulted me about putting a dredge on it. After every aspect of the question had been thrashed out, it was decided that though the method would very likely prove the best under all the circumstances, the machine would have to enter via the St. Michael route, and so reach Dawson too late the first season to do more than arrange to have it hauled by sleighs to the field, where most of the work of putting together the machinery would have to be done; this coming in, in parts small enough to be handled by men. This, together with the enormous freight rates of that time, would pile up the cost of even a medium capacity machine to a practically prohibitive sum, and the idea was abandoned, never to be taken up again by the same persons.

In the summer of 1898 a personal friend of my own, the late Mr. John A. McPherson, who was associated with a Cincinnati capitalist, Mr. Hines, brought the machinery and lumber for the construction of a small dredge over the White Pass Railway, which had just been completed, to the head of Lake Bennett, and from there by the Cañon route to the lease-holds owned by them on the Lewes River, extending some distance above the mouth of the Big Salmon. Notwithstanding all the difficulties confronting Mr. McPherson, the material was all safely landed, the hull constructed, launched, machinery erected, and the dredge at work the first week in September, which is something of a record. As is usual in such ventures, under new and largely unknown conditions, it took all the remainder of the season to get the machine adjusted to its environment.

Mr. McPherson was on his way back to the field the following spring, but he met with a serious accident on the coast, and had to return to his home after a stay in the hospital. His associate, Mr. Hines, came in, but after running the dredge for a short time near Big Salmon River, he was, I was informed, taken sick, and becoming disheartened, ordered the machine downstream to be sold or returned to the builders. At Dawson it was arranged with some parties there to place it on one of the claims on lower Bonanza. It was dismantled and hauled by wagon to claim No. 42 below discovery, where it was set up, and though the ground was frozen from the surface down to bedrock, it worked it out in less than two seasons, with profit to both machine owners and claim owners.

It was then moved up to discovery claim, which it worked over again after it was worked out by the hand system. The ground here was thawed by steam to save wear and tear of the dredge and increase its output, and though this is expensive, it was continued, showing that it must have paid. The owners of the dredge also purchased from our friend Skookum Jim the remains of his claim, No. I above discovery, after he had worked on it about six years, paying for it sixty thousand dollars, which shows, perhaps, more forcibly than anything else that could be said, the thoroughness of dredging as compared with the old system of firing and sluicing, by which Jim principally worked.

Dredging, like hydrosluicing, requires a lot of money to begin it properly, so much that it cannot be counted available to any but the wealthy or a company. A medium sized machine when put to work in the most accessible parts of the Yukon Territory will cost from sixty to seventy-five thousand dollars. A larger one will cost proportionally more, depending on the weight of metal in the machinery and the amount of lumber in the hull and house. Something, too, depends on the quality of metal in the working parts. It is safe to state that a machine, of say 250 cubic yards capacity per hour, not a very large one as they go now, will cost not less than one hundred thousand dollars in the most advantageously situated parts of the Yukon Territory, that is at points on the main tributaries, like the Hootalinqua, Pelly, or Stewart, or even on the main stream itself. If the material has to be hauled far from the main arteries, the cost may be doubled or even trebled, depending on the distance and difficulties.

It is very evident then that the prospector has not much show to make anything by this method, unless he is prepared to give the lion's share to someone who will provide a dredge. Here, too, he is handicapped by the regulations which require the payment of one hundred dollars per mile of river bed, sixty days after his application is filed. He is allowed to acquire ten miles, and has to pay down one thousand dollars. He is required to put on a dredge to be approved by the Minister of the Interior within three years of the issuance of his lease, and to pay ten dollars per mile each subsequent year of the existence of his leasehold. Now it will take more than one season to thoroughly prospect the ground, and if he begins prospecting before making application, he is at the mercy of anyone who may deem it good enough to acquire. The sixty days after application will hardly enable one to get the necessary appliances for prospecting to the ground. The drill alone required to make the necessary tests will cost about three thousand dollars laid down at Whitehorse, and take a month to get there, and it may cost nearly as much and take more time to get it from there to the ground desired.

After the ground is selected, all that can be done in the sixty days between the date of application and the payment of the money is to make a very superficial examination which may be very misleading in its results; the prospects on the surface being good, but nothing beneath, there is no way to tell differently till a drill has thoroughly and systematically prospected the leasehold from surface to bedrock, unless the latter should prove to be at an impracticable depth, in which case the test would have to be limited to a practical digging depth for a dredge. This depth may be modified by conditions that can be learned only through the work of the drill. The minimum width allowed for a dredging stream is one hundred and fifty feet, all under that being reserved for placer mining.

Let us assume that we have a leasehold ten miles long, and varying from two to three hundred feet wide. Such a stretch of ground ought to have at least a pair of drill holes at intervals of five hundred feet, and this would not give a too conclusive test. Under the most favorable circumstances two holes a week would be good work, which takes into consideration moving the drill, and all other contingencies. Ten miles would require in this not too critical examination two hundred and ten holes, which would take one hundred weeks, and as the most favorable season there affords not more than twenty-two, we see that it would require five seasons to complete the prospect, and the applicant has to go it blind altogether too much. True he may have learned from other sources something of the nature of the locality he is in, but in the case of a pioneer, or pioneers, that is not likely.

Clarence J. Berry and Wife
John W. Leonard

Perhaps the most romantic story is that of Clarence J. Berry and his wife "the bride of the Klondike." Mr. Berry was a fruit raiser in Fresno Country, California. He found it a hard task to make a living there. In 1894 he heard of gold finds in the Yukon region, in far-off Alaska. He had just $40 of his own and managed to borrow $60 more on the promise of heavy interest. He went to Juneau, where he found a number of others who had arrived there with the view of crossing over the mountains. A party of forty was organized, among whom was Berry. It was early spring, when they started out each with a load of supplies and furs. Indians packed these to the top of the Chilkoot Pass. The winter journey in the mountains proved too much for many in the party and many gave up in despair and turned back. When the lakes were reached and boats built the water voyage was begun. The melted snow had swollen the streams, and in Lake Bennett the whole outfit of supplies went down. This discouraged all but three. Berry, with magnificent strength and a hero's courage, was one of the three who with a meager supply of food pushed on, and after nearly a month's toilsome journey reached Forty-Mile Creek, penniless. He went to work for others and later for himself, with indifferent success, but acquired a faith in future fortune on the Yukon which made him determined to find it or die in the attempt. In the fall of 1895 he concluded to return to Selma, Fresno Country, where he had left a young woman who had promised to be his wife. When he returned he found Miss Ethel D. Bush prepared not only to redeem her promise but also to go with him and share his fortunes in the frozen North, although he pictured to her the hardships as well as the hopes that belonged to life in that region. In March, 1896, they were married, and in April the couple reached Juneau on their unique wedding trip. They had little capital, but two brave hearts. They went by boat to Dyea, the head of navigation, and from there over the mountains by dog team. At night they slept under a tent on a bed of boughs. Mrs. Berry's garments resembled her husband's. They were made of seal fur with the fur inside, and came over her feet like old-fashioned sandals. Over them were pulled a pair of gum boots. Over her shoulders was a fur robe and her hood was of bearskin. This all made a great weight of clothing, but she trudged by her husband's side, and in June, three months after they were married, they reached the camp at Forty-Mile Creek. There Berry worked until in September, 1896, he was told of McCormack's find up the Klondike. There was much excitement at "Forty-Mile" over the news, though the experienced miners for the most part ridiculed the idea that anything good would be found "over there on the Klondike." Berry, however, was one of those who believed that something good had been found, and his wife helped him to get ready for his trip into the new district, Mrs. Berry remaining at Forty-Mile. Two days later, Berry was in the Bonanza district, where it had been decided that 500 feet on the river Bonanza Creek should constitute a claim. His location was "Claim No. 40 above the Discovery" — which means that thirty-nine 500-foot claims intervened between his ground and the original one staked out by George McCormack.

On El Dorado Creek

Soon Mrs. Berry went to Dawson City, which had just been started. Mr. Berry built a house, and was joined by his wife. He secured Claim No.5 above the Discovery on El Dorado Creek and there found rich dirt varying from $2 to the pan just below the surface to $50 to the pan on the bedrock. Mr. Berry hired men at $15 a day and from the $130,000 which he took out before he left he paid out $22,000 to his miners. He still owns his claims on the Bonanza and El Dorado, besides interest in many others, and has a fortune which will reach into the millions. Mrs. Berry will remain in Fresno, but Mr. Berry will return to manage his mines, which he left in good hands to be worked during his absence. Mr. Berry's El Dorado claim was one of the richest that had been worked on the creek during the winter and spring. The principal part of his $130,000 came from thirty "box-lengths" of dirt. A "box-length" is fifteen feet long and twelve feet wide. In one length he found a pocket of $10,000. In another length was a nugget weighing thirteen ounces — next to the largest found in the diggings.

Refuse work at $1.25 per hour

All winter men received $1.25 an hour on the Berry claim, but at these wages not a pick would have been raised had it not been for the fact that nothing can be done during the severe cold but pile the gravel on the dump ready for washing in the spring, and many of these men did not have enough food to keep them at this work on their own claims. Every day was pay day. Mr. Berry settled with his men every night merely by taking a pan of dirt, washing it out with water obtained from melted ice, and weighting out each man's time in gold nuggets. His expenses averaged from $100 to $150 a day all winter, but this was a small sum for a place whence every man expects to return home a millionaire, and where a man with less than $50 in his dust sack is looked upon as broke.

Although Mr. Berry is proud of his plucky wife he did not give her a cent of "pin money" out of his riches while they were on the Klondike. He did not need to do so; for in the intervals of house-keeping she would go to the dump and wash out a few pans of dirt for herself. In this way she secured over $10,000 as her personal perquisites for sixteen months of a bridal "outing" in the frozen Northwest.

The Call of the Wild
Robert Service

Have you gazed on naked grandeur
   where there's nothing else to gaze on,
 Set pieces and drop-curtain scenes galore,
Big mountains heaved to heaven,
   which the blinding sunsets blazon,
 Black canyons where the rapids rip and roar?
Have you swept the visioned valley
   with the green stream streaking through it,
 Searched the Vastness for a something you have lost?
Have you strung your soul to silence?
   Then for God's sake go and do it;
 Hear the challenge, learn the lesson, pay the cost.

Have you wandered in the wilderness,
   the sagebrush desolation,
 The bunch-grass levels where the cattle graze?
Have you whistled bits of ragtime
   at the end of all creation,
 And learned to know the desert's little ways?
Have you camped upon the foothills,
   have you galloped o'er the ranges,
 Have you roamed the arid sun-lands
   through and through?
Have you chummed up with the mesa?
   Do you know its moods and changes?
 Then listen to the Wild —it's calling you.

Have you known the Great White Silence,
   not a snow-gemmed twig aquiver?
 (Eternal truths that shame our soothing lies.)
Have you broken trail on snowshoes,
   mushed your huskies up the river,

Dared the unknown, led the way,
      and clutched the prize?
Have you marked the map's void spaces,
       mingled with the mongrel races,
  Felt the savage strength of brute in every thew?
And though grim as hell the worst is,
      can you round it off with curses?
  Then hearken to the Wild — it's wanting you.

Have you suffered, starved, and triumphed,
      groveled down, yet grasped at glory,
  Grown bigger in the bigness of the whole?
"Done things" just for the doing,
      letting babblers tell the story,
  Seeing through the nice veneer the naked soul?
Have you seen God in His splendors,
      heard the text that nature renders—
  (You'll never hear it in the family pew.)
The simple things, the true things,
      the silent men who do things?
  Then listen to the Wild — it's calling you.

They have cradled you in custom,
      they have primed you with their preaching,
  They have soaked you in convention
      through and through;
They have put you in a showcase;
      you're a credit to their teaching.
  But can't you hear the Wild? — it's calling you.

Let us probe the silent places,
      let us seek what luck betides us;
  Let us journey to a lonely land I know.
There's a whisper on the night-wind,
      there's a star agleam to guide us,
  And the Wild is calling, calling…let us go.

Paris of the North

Dawson sprang almost instantly from the swampy muskeg at the confluence of the Yukon and Klondike rivers. It was a true boom town with a heyday that lasted only a year or two. At its peak Dawson had a population of more than 40,000 and was the largest Canadian city west of Winnipeg. It was a tent town with numerous clapboard dance halls, casinos and saloons.

Most stampeders arrived in Dawson in the spring and summer of 1898. They wandered into this carnival-like town exhausted from their arduous trek. There are many stories of stampeders who upon arriving in Dawson immediately booked passage home, so travel weary and worn-out they did not have any energy to even try to work a claim.

Most of the population of Dawson dined on beans and pancakes. They slept in canvas tents and spent their days in idle anticipation of finding their fortune. They had endured the most arduous and difficult experience of their life just getting to the Klondike valley. Now they were idle with little opportunity to stake or even work someone's claim.

The irony of the Klondike Gold Rush was that the gold fields had been almost entirely staked the year before the stampeders arrived. There was little opportunity for day laborers and many stampeders were flat broke. Dawson was a boom town where the fabulously rich and the dirt poor walked the same wooden planks over the marshy streets. Despair was everywhere except in the dance halls, saloons and shops.

For a short time Dawson was the 'Paris of the North' and had a range of goods and services that haven't been seen since. In Dawson you could buy the best champagne and sip it in fine crystal. You could dine on filet mignon, oysters and caviar. Fine silks, jewelry and gowns were available for a price. Virtually anything was possible in Dawson.

It was a town of rich contradictions. The North West Mounted Police maintained a close rein on the town. The police freely sentenced people to the police barracks woodpile or, in the case of more serious offenses, banished the convicted from the Klondike valley. Prostitutes could pursue their trade openly, and gambling halls held freedoms beyond anything seen on the continent. On the other hand, certain laws were enforced with great fervor. For instance, carrying guns was strictly forbidden and may have been the reason there was not a single murder in Dawson during the first hectic summer. On Sundays and certain holidays the town came screeching to a halt. Every saloon, dance hall and casino closed their doors from midnight Saturday until midnight Sunday. In the midst of the chaos Dawson was silenced. Work of any kind was not permitted, and more than one person was fined for chopping wood on Sunday.

Dawson in the Midst of the Boom
Arthur T. Walden

The town of Dawson had undergone tremendous changes since I saw it last. The whole riverfront now for half a mile was tier upon tier of boats, scows, and rafts, so that a man landing on the edge of this mass of boats would have to cross possibly a dozen or more before getting on shore. A good proportion of the people were still living on their boats. The river was in flood at the time. It was only the big eddy that sets back in front of Dawson that saved all these boats from breaking away and being swept down the river in a body. The town itself was a swirling mass of humanity. The main street was nothing but a sea of mud, and the packhorses and mules were always getting stuck in it. The buildings were almost entirely of canvas, consisting of tents for smaller uses and canvas-covered frames for larger purposes. Saloons, dance halls, and gambling-halls were the chief industry. But the North-West Mounted Police had charge and gave us a good government.

The town was the most unsanitary place imaginable. I know a man who made a bet that he could go down the main street and travel the whole way jumping from one dead horse to another or to a dead dog, and he won his bet. The latter part of the summer typhoid began to rage and there were often eight or ten deaths a day. There was only one cow in town and she died, leaving the patients with only condensed milk.

A good many medical men had arrived in the country for one reason or another. No doctor could practice in Canada without an examination and license from the Government at Ottawa, so they got around this by all turning nurses. This typhoid raged until the freeze-up. Men came in from the outlying creeks for a few days, and returning carried the disease back and died in their camps, often alone. I found a cabin the following year, almost a hundred miles up the Klondike River, with two men dead in it, and as they had died in their bunks and had plenty of food we presumed their deaths must have been from typhoid.

We had only a few cases of scurvy. As this had always been more or less prevalent before, we laid its abatement to the greater variety of food. It was claimed that a man never got it after he had been there two years, but whether this is universally true or not I cannot say. I never heard of dog-drivers having it, and they certainly lived more roughly than any one else.

The mines didn't really get into full swing until almost a year later. A friend of mine discovered a salt lick about ten miles up a side creek of the Yukon, moved his camp up there, and hunted moose for the market. He always made his headquarters with us when he came to town, and used to give us the moose nose, which is considered the daintiest part of the moose. This we used to skin and boil whole for several hours, and then soak it in vinegar. It was a great delicacy. This man eventually starved to death. Some men coming down the river stopped at the mouth of his creek and walked up to his camp, where they found him dead in his blankets, and not a bit of food in the camp. Investigation showed that he had had scurvy and then starved to death. Scurvy affects the legs first, and he had dragged himself around the camp till he got too weak to do even that.

The first trip I took up the creeks after getting back, I lugged a large Colt revolver and cartridge belt with me, in case I should see a moose. On my way down I got sick of packing the thing and strapped it onto a large dog I had with me. No one in that country would have thought it a strange sight, but when I got down to Dawson, a boat that had just arrived was tying up at the wharf, and a man yelled out, "For Heaven's sake, Bill, come and look what sort of a country we've got into! The dogs are carrying six-shooters!" When they spoke of it I noticed the swagger that the dog seemed to put on, and didn't wonder at the exclamation of the Cheechako. Queen Victoria's birthday was celebrated that spring by every one. As the summer crept on and the Fourth of July approached, an ugly rumor got started, from I don't know where, that the Mounted Police were not going to allow the Americans to celebrate it. The Americans outnumbered the Canadians about fifteen to one, as every one who wasn't a Canadian said he was American. We swore we would celebrate in spite of everything. Nothing was noticeable as the time drew near except the excessive politeness of the Americans and Canadians toward each other. We all knew that if the

Mounted Police said we shouldn't celebrate they meant it, but we determined to celebrate anyway. It was an extremely difficult proposition to handle, and a very nasty undercurrent was running in the camp.

After the rumor had got started, the Mounted Police knew that, if they didn't say anything about it and allowed us to celebrate, it would be said that they were afraid to stop us. If they said that the Americans could celebrate, it would amount to the same thing. A few days before the Fourth a proclamation came out, signed by Colonel Steele, the commanding officer, written almost in the language of a command, saying that the Americans and Canadians would celebrate the Fourth of July together. You might call this tact. When the Fourth arrived, all that we did in the way of gunplay was to shoot each other's stovepipes off. Later in the day various sports were held and the greatest good will prevailed. The only things that seemed to suffer were the dogs, and the town was full of them; they simply went mad with fright, running in every direction. My team disappeared completely, with the exception of one dog which I found under my bunk twenty-four hours afterwards. Some of the dogs never turned up at all.

The town was now building at a tremendous rate, and all of logs. Everybody was trying to get his cabin or other building finished before the cold weather set in. Rafts of logs were coming down the river all the time, and two sawmills were working overtime. Large pack trains were constantly going out to the mines with provisions, and a crude suspension bridge was thrown over the Klondike River. Restaurants, stores, theaters, dance-halls, and of course gambling-halls and saloons, were going full blast.

The saloons were almost like clubrooms, patronized alike by temperance men and drinkers. The custom now began among the saloonkeepers of shutting down for a few hours or days while they made minor changes or repairs. Then they would hold what was called a "Grand Opening," and everybody seemed to patronize them the more to help them recover from the time when they were closed. But with all this activity there didn't seem to be the insane feverishness that you meet in a large city.

An incident happened the next winter which I think I shall mention here in connection with the Dawson saloons. One very popular saloonkeeper had a "Grand Opening" which was, you might say, too successful, because he was so well patronized that they drank up all his available whiskey. Being a man who could rise to an emergency, and seeing that he was losing trade, he made a speech to the gathering, something like this:

"Gentlemen: I opened to-night with the expectation that I could give a good welcome and plenty of refreshments to my friends. But fate is against me. I have twelve dog-teams coming down the river, which are expected today, loaded to the gunwale with the finest whiskey that man ever drank.

"You remember when I was out last summer I visited my old home in Kentucky. As a boy a legend floated around there of a hidden cave, way back in the times of the Civil War, which was raided by the Government officials, and a hundred and forty barrels of whiskey were found in it. The distillers themselves were killed in the fight, and the heads of the hundred and forty barrels were stove in, and this priceless fluid was spilled on the floor of the cave. The cave's mouth was then roughly rocked up, and soon overgrown with the verdure of that country, and in those harrowing times when men's hearts bled and women's tears ran, all trace and memory of the cave was lost.

"By chance a boy, a rabbit hunter, chasing his fleeting game through this howling wilderness, saw his prey disappear into these deep rocks, and being a boy and knowing that he would get a licking from his father if he didn't get the rabbit, he pried out some of the rocks and discovered the cave of the legend. This was done just when I got back to Kentucky. And, gentlemen, those hundred and forty barrels of whiskey spilled on the barren rocks of the cave had drained into a hollow, and there by evaporating for some forty years had reduced down in the sterilized air of the cave to only ten barrels, and I, gentlemen, bought every drop of it, and am now having it shipped to the brave men of the Yukon.

"Now, gentlemen, my dog-teams are somewhere on the ice, if they are not under it, but rather than disappoint you I will give you a little of my private stock, which I scooped out with my own hands from the deepest depression of the pocket. This, gentlemen, I will give you to-night at the same reduced price you have always paid."

With that he turned to one of his bartenders, who was wearing a broad grin, and said, "Johnny, bring in my private stock." The bartender, rising to the occasion, dipped two buckets of Yukon water out of a barrel, produced several demijohns of alcohol and different ingredients, and made his whiskey before our eyes. It must have been pure because we all saw it done, and what's more, everybody went up and had a drink to see what the stuff did taste like. But I don't think any saloonkeeper in the place but Pete Macdonald could have got away with it.

At this time I saw an example of the unique way of advertising that some men practiced up there, and how earnestly it was taken by the men who came in contact with it. One of the large restaurants came out with the old story that had been told a great many times in the North, with many variations, that a mastodon had been found in an underground glacier, in a perfect state of preservation, and how the bones and hide were being shipped out to the Smithsonian Institution. This particular restaurant was said to have bought all the flesh, and was serving it a dollar and a half a plate. What they were really serving was simply first-class beefsteak. They also backed up this article in the newspaper by a large notice on their bills of fare: "Fresh Mastodon Steak Today."

An old-timer coming down from the creeks, where he had been for over a year, asked where was the best place to get a good feed, and a friend showed him the article in the paper and advised him to try it. The old-timer went to the restaurant and called for mastodon steak, which by this time had become a regular order of the patrons. After getting the steak and trying a mouthful, he remarked to the waiter that it tasted like beef. The waiter, having got sick of this mastodon business and not seeing the joke of it anyway, said, "You damned fool, what do you expect?" Whereupon the old-timer rose in his wrath and said he had ordered mastodon steak, which they had advertised, and mastodon steak he would have or nothing, and stamped out, mad all through.

Almost from the very beginning of the rush there had been a constant buying and selling of claims. A great many of these were bought and sold without anything being known about their contents beyond their proximity to good or bad claims. As the saying goes, "Gold is where you find it."

It is a fact, of course, that the pay streak in a claim that had only a few prospect holes in it and appeared to be a big find might suddenly stop, or, on the other hand, a poor one might turn into a rich one. Later on people grew wiser, and claims were thoroughly prospected and holes made in many places so that a good guess could be made as to their richness. A half-interest in one claim I know of was sold for a hundred dollars, and afterwards turned out to be worth half a million. Another claim was sold to a man for two thousand dollars, as this was all the money he had, and this turned out to be one of the very richest of the Klondike. This man panned out ten thousand dollars worth of gold in his mud-box during the winter, and gave it to the man who had sold him the claim, with the remark: "When you have spent all this you can come back and get a job on your old claim." Of course "salting" was practiced, too, with more or less success.

There was a man here whom I presume that everybody at the time had heard of, called "Swift Water Bill." This man, when I first met him, was in the Birch Creek district, digging out the only habitation he owned on earth, a tent, which had fallen down and been overrun by a glacier. As far as I know he didn't have a cent in the world. But as luck would have it he staked a very rich claim in the Klondike. Immediately he began to improve himself in dress. By picking up a piece here and a piece there he was soon garbed like a civilized man, and could have passed very well in a city; though having only one shirt he had to go to bed while it was being washed. I think he had the distinction of wearing the first white collar in the Yukon.

He soon became engaged to a girl in town but they had some tiff, and to take it out on him she went to a restaurant on the arm of a gambler. Swift Water Bill was sitting in the restaurant near the door, and heard her say she would like some eggs. Now these eggs were the first that had come into the Yukon Valley. The entire lot had been bought by the restaurant-keeper and were being served at a dollar-fifty apiece. Swift Water Bill, being no fool, sent for the proprietor before the gambler had a chance to get in his order, and bought every egg in the house. As they brought him relays of fried eggs, he flipped them out of the window to the waiting dogs outside, with remarks to the crowd in general on the smartness of the dogs in catching them. This little episode cost him six hundred dollars, but the girl came back to him.

This time, though, she married him, helped him to spend all his money, and got a divorce from him. Again with his luck he struck another good claim, and married a sister of the first girl. This was repeated with a third sister. His first two wives were on the stage, acting in a play called "Still Water Willie." Swift Water Bill used to go and see himself caricatured, and applaud louder than any one.

During the winter, when the gold was being got out from his claim under the charge of a foreman, Swift Water Bill stayed in Dawson. As the gold-bearing diggings were thrown on a dump, frozen, and were not available till the next spring, Swift Water borrowed money to gamble with at ten per cent a month, which was the usual rate of interest of the country.

He became a famous gambler, and was very fond of hiring a faro table for the evening, when his customary remark before beginning was, "Gentlemen, the limit is from the floor to the ceiling," which meant that there was no limit. Any one can beat a faro bank if only he has money enough, provided there is no limit, by doubling his bets. Various little flurries took place that were well worth watching. It was interesting to see a man, dirty and unkempt, with earth-stained clothes, lose ten to twenty thousand dollars at one sitting. Gambling has always been thought of in a mining camp as connected with shooting and fighting of all kinds, but here I don't remember one gambling fight that amounted to anything. The gambling halls were orderly, well conducted, and on the square. This I think was entirely due to the North-West Mounted Police, who were always in evidence. They allowed things to go without interference to a certain limit. After that they stepped in.

The dance halls also were orderly, and generally had two policemen lounging around, apparently not taking the least notice of anything. But toward morning, when the better element had gone and things began to get rougher, the policemen were always Johnny-on-the-spot. I saw a case where a man, running to catch a girl, pushed a policeman out of his way, not knowing who he was, and threw him in a heap in a corner. The policeman was on his feet in a second and after the man, but was grabbed by his fellow constable and they both laughed, knowing that no insult was meant.

Sometimes in the midst of the noise and uproar a man's voice would ring out in a different tone, and all the dancers would fall away from two men somewhere in the hall. But instantly there would be a policeman at their side and the thing would be settled without any trouble. The individual dances lasted for three minutes each and cost a dollar, paid to the man at the bar. With this a drink was included. The girls got twenty-five per cent of the money for each dance, and some of them made as much as twenty-five dollars a night.

These girls as a general thing were professional dancers. Some of them were married women who were escorted to the dance halls by their husbands, danced all night, and were then escorted home by them. The girls were always dressed in the height of fashion and danced in slippers, not moccasins. I never saw any real rowdyism at these dances. Occasionally a couple would get up and give a fancy dance, usually an impromptu affair, and some of them were certainly wonderful. The men were dressed in everything from the attire of civilization down to the Siwash garb, but no one ever knew from the looks of a man's clothes how much money he had.

The theaters were good, bad, and indifferent. We had a troupe that was wintering there, and they gave a series of old plays that were really very well done. Of course "Uncle Tom's Cabin" had to be given. I have seen this several times in my life, but I never saw the parts of Eliza and Simon Legree so well done. I can't say as much for the pack of bloodhounds. These were represented by a Malamute puppy, drawn across the stage in a sitting posture by an invisible wire and yelling his full displeasure to the gods. The ice was represented by newspapers. Eliza acted her part exceptionally well on the newspapers, having seen people actually cross floating ice.

Among some of the interesting people whom I met at this time was a girl who had come in over the ice that winter, with two dogs. She was the only true "cowgirl" I have ever met, although I have seen a good many imitations. She was born and bred in the West and had run her own ranch in Alberta, taken care of her mother, and taught school. She was independent, fearless, and intelligent, and on top of it all was extremely good-looking and could have made her way in any walk of life. This girl had come into the country alone, stopping at the Mounted Police posts on the way down. She hired the cabin next to ours in Dawson and immediately started to acquire some mining property. She was, I think, the most remarkable horse-woman I have ever known.

One day she wanted me to go with her and show her some mining property she wanted to buy, and she asked me to get her a good horse. I selected the best horse I could find in town. On the way to her cabin the horse and I had a difference of opinion, in which the horse won out. Thinking myself something of a rider, I had misgivings about offering her this horse, but I changed my mind when I saw her get onto it.

I was walking, and in the rough places I got ahead of the horse. We kept passing and repassing each other for the first ten miles up the Klondike River. At this point there was a horse-ferry. One of the down-river scows had been brought up and attached to a tight wire cable stretched across the river at some little distance above the water. There were two pulleys on the cable, from one of which a rope ran to the bow of the scow, while from the other a rope ran to the stern. By tightening or slackening these ropes the proper cant was given to the ferry, so that it was carried across the river by the force of the current.

These scows were decked fore and aft for about eight feet. The horses were taken onto the forward deck by a narrow gangplank and thus into the cockpit. The river being swift and deep near the bank it was a ticklish business getting them aboard.

When we arrived at the ferry two Englishmen were trying to get their horses into the scow. They had taken the packs off and with a great deal of handling and talking to the horses they managed to get them over the plank and down into the cockpit. Miss Howe sat on her horse, waiting for them to get out of her way, with a rather amused expression. When everything was clear she literally seemed to lift her horse by the spurs to the middle of the gangplank, which buckled badly with the impact, but the next jump was made onto the deck of the scow, where she rode him down into the cockpit, and swung off, throwing the reins over the horse's head for me to hold. I don't think any of us got our eyes and mouths closed till we reached the other bank. There the process was reversed.

Before this ferry had been installed, a bateau used to be run here in the same way. One day several men came down with their packs on their backs to be taken across. They all took their packs off with the exception of one man, whose pack was fastened so tight that he couldn't remove it. As ill luck would have it, the ferryboat tipped over. Everybody was saved (except the one man whose pack was so heavy that it sank him.

About this time we had an epidemic of something around town that resembled grippe. Among others Miss Howe came down with it. The doctor who came to see her told us she ought to have some means of communication with us if she was taken sick in the night. One of us rigged up a small rope that ran from her bed through the wall of her cabin, across the alley to ours, then through our wall and across our floor to the wall beyond, where it was hitched to a dog-harness with bells on it. The idea was that if she needed anything and pulled the rope in the night, the dog-harness would drop down and the bells would wake us up.

There was no signal until some time in the middle of the night, when with a bang and a rattle of bells the harness dropped to the floor, scooted across it and up the other wall. We all woke up with a jump, thinking that the girl must be terribly ill. Getting on what clothes we could, we rushed around to her door, banging on it until a voice sang out from the interior, "I don't know who you men are, but if you aren't gone in one second I'm going to shoot!"

Explanations followed and upon examination we found that a man had gone through the alley, caught on the rope and pulled it along with him accidentally, giving the alarm, but not disturbing the girl. I heard later on that she married one of the North-West Mounted Police.

This summer a little incident happened which showed what nerve some men have, and illustrated their fortitude in standing pain. Three of us had dropped down the river in a poling boat, and had the misfortune to get caught in a logjam, where most of the current swept under the logs. In trying to save our boat from being drawn under, one of the men had the ill luck to break his leg between the knee and ankle. The question then arose what to do about it, as it would take two or three days to get him up to Dawson.

At his suggestion we decided to set it ourselves. It was the big shin-bone that was broken, and the ends had slipped and gone by each other. None of us knew anything about surgery, but we had some common sense. So after a good deal of discussion, in which he

joined almost as impartially as we did, he was lashed in a sitting posture with his back against a tree, blankets being used so that the
ropes wouldn't cut him. Then some sacks were wrapped around his
ankle and a rope wound around these, coming from either side so
as to get a direct pull and not to cant the ankle.

The ends of the rope were hitched to a long lever which was put
around a tree. Two of us on this lever managed, by hauling steadily
and evenly, to pull the lower end of his leg down so that the other
man could work the ends of the bones back together and hold them
in position, binding splints in place. With the exception of spitting
a good deal of tobacco juice, the man didn't show the least indication of pain. Several times afterwards we made him exhibit his leg
in a dance hall to show what a good job we had done.

I saw an amusing incident this summer. My cabin was just below
one of the trails. Back of it and above the trail was another dog-dri-
ver's cabin. Farther down this trail were camped two men who had
just come into the country and were living in a tent. One evening
a pair of horses came walking by that had been hauling logs back of
the town. They came down loose and singly, with their chain traces
hooked back onto their breeching. As they walked along, the other
driver's dogs jumped them, starting them into a trot. Hereupon the
trace of one of the horses came loose and caught in the ridgepole
of the tent. The tent was caught up like a tablecloth, and both horses stampeded down the trail with the tent following them.

The two strangers had been eating their dinner inside the tent,
with the grub-box as table. When the tent was whisked away they
were suddenly brought into publicity. As they chased their tent full-
speed down the trail, after the runaway horse, the dogs quit the pursuit of the horse and piled into the unfinished dinner. The men
soon came back with the rescued tent, but found a new disaster, as
the marauding dogs had not only cleaned up their dinner but
robbed their grub-box as well.

After the atmosphere had cleared up a little and the men could
appreciate a bit of humor, I invited them down to my cabin, to give
them what hospitality I could. One of them then informed me that
it was an unlucky tent anyway, as it had already been through the
great snow-slide on Chilkoot Pass, and they thought they had better get rid of it or it might involve them in another catastrophe.

There was a famous old-timer here at this time. He had made a trail that cattle and horses could be taken over, spending a good deal of time and money on it, and this trail was named the Dalton Trail after him. He was one of the men who had helped to make Alaska. About this time, or perhaps a little later, I heard a story of a party of men arriving with some beef cattle, intending to drive them over the Dalton Trail. They were advised by some of the people on the coast to get Dalton's permission: this he was always glad to give, along with help in the way of sketch-maps. The asking for permission was only a matter of courtesy. Their reply was that this was a free country and they guessed they would travel that trail whether he was willing or not.

Dalton heard of this. The morning they pulled out with their cattle he appeared, mounted, with his six-shooter and rifle, and calmly informed them that he was going along with them the entire journey. Furthermore, he announced they would be allowed to use the trail where it went through canyons or across fords, where there was no other place to pass; but anywhere else, if man or beast stepped onto that trail he would kill him. I believe the trail is over two hundred and ninety miles long. Dalton rode the entire distance with them, traveling on his own trail and seeing that they kept off. Where it joined the Yukon he turned around and rode back to the coast.

All this summer boats kept coming. Prices of food dropped steadily until you could buy supplies almost at Seattle prices. The market was filled, too, because many discouraged men were selling their outfits and leaving for the outside. The mines that could be worked in summer were in full blast. Prospectors were swarming all over the hills and creeks. I spent part of the summer on Last Chance Creek, where Kronstadt and I had a claim. A few cabins had been built on this creek and men were busy prospecting and getting ready for winter.

In the course of the summer a man killed his partner on Last Chance Creek, shut himself in his cabin, and swore that he would kill any man who came near. Work was stopped on the creek and a man was sent the eighteen miles to Dawson to inform the Mounted Police, since they would not permit us to take the law into our own hands. Eventually a lone policeman showed up.

Upon his arrival we asked him when they were coming up to arrest the man, as we were tired of keeping watch over the cabin. The policeman's reply was that the colonel had sent him up to get the man. We then told him that the man had shut himself in his cabin, swearing that he would shoot the first man who came near him, and that it was certain death to go within range.

These cabins were built of logs, with a foot or more of dirt on the roof, and were almost impregnable. These were the days of black powder when the old forty-fives didn't have the penetrating power of the newer guns. So this man's cabin was really a first-class fort. All that he needed to do to make a loophole was to poke some moss out between the logs.

After sitting there some little time and smoking a cigarette, the policeman said he guessed he'd have to make a try at it. Getting up, stiff from his long walk up to the mines through the mud, he went over toward the cabin. When about fifty feet from the door he put on a military bearing, walked up, and knocked on the door, calling, "Open in the Queen's name." We all expected to see him shot down, knowing what sort of man was inside.

Every gun of the watchers was turned on the door. Police or no police, law or no law, I think every man intended to shoot the occupant if the policeman were killed. Much to our surprise the door was thrown open and the man appeared unarmed, his shoulders square, his head a little on one side, not in the least dejected-looking, and held out his wrists to be handcuffed. The policeman had not drawn his gun. Feeling around for the bracelets, apparently not watching the man, the officer handcuffed him.

The whole thing was done with about as much spectacular display as if the policeman had been looking for a piece of string to tie a dog with. Not a word was said, as far as I know, until we began to crowd around the pair. Then the prisoner, speaking to the policeman and ignoring us, said to him in a voice loud enough to be heard by all, "Sir, I watched you from the time you started to come up to my cabin, and had you covered, simply waiting till you got near enough so I couldn't miss you, I had every intention of killing you, knowing my own life was forfeited. But I found it impossible to shoot down in cold blood a man who was braver than I. However, I should have liked to get in a few shots at these blankety-blank cowards who had me surrounded, only they were hardly worth it." He said a good deal more to our discredit than this.

The policeman got red in the face and looked uncomfortable. Then, taking his man, he started back on the long walk to Dawson. This was the method of the North-West Mounted Police: one man for a man. But they had the majesty of the English law back of them. We went back to work after they had gone, and I guess we all felt rather small.

This was the open season for tall stories of every description from the outlying country. Some men claimed to have found the "mother lode" of gold. One man was said to have shot a musk ox, never seen in this country, but when the story was run down it turned out that he had eaten a muskrat.

Another found a new-fangled kind of tent, of a dark blue color, floating down the Klondike, and word went round that it was André's balloon that had drifted across the North Pole and had never been heard from.

One old-timer, Hank Summers, one of the best liars that ever lived, had left for the outside. As usual with us he went busted, and wondered how he could get back to the Yukon. Chancing to meet on the train a professor of archaeology, who was very much interested in the discovery of mastodon remains in Alaska, Hank told the timeworn story of finding a mastodon buried in an underground glacier.

The professor was very much interested and a bargain was struck by which he would pay Hank's passage back into the country if Hank would send him the skin and bones of the mastodon after he got there. Hank wondered all the way in how he was going to pay his debt. But he soon forgot his troubles. When he arrived in the country and found that a claim that he owned had turned out well and had made him a rich man for life, he forgot his worries about mastodons. He worked all summer, sold his claim in the fall, and left on the last boat out; with no mastodon.

But all the way down the river, whenever the boat stopped, whether at a white village or an Eskimo, he bought mastodon bones, tusks, and teeth, until he had a sizable hoard collected in the fore part of the steamer. This he shipped to the said professor, and we hope he was satisfied. The country at that time was full of mastodon bones, which the Indians collected and sold to the white men. The miners discovered a good many in the mines as well.

A huge mastodon molar, weighing eighteen and a quarter pounds and in a perfect state of preservation, was "hocked" to a man named Harris by a chap who soon afterwards disappeared. This molar was a beautiful dark mahogany color, and I was very anxious to get it for a paperweight for a dentist friend of mine. Harris wouldn't sell it. But since he was an old man and a great drunkard as well, I hoped that he would soon die and I should be able to get the tooth. Unfortunately when this happened I was three hundred miles away and some other chap got it instead.

.

Saloons
Tappan Adney

I heard a man say Dawson was the first place he was ever in where it was no disgrace to be "dead broke." Gold dust was, of course, the medium of exchange. But the profits of mine-owners and the wages of workmen, amounting to millions, were frozen fast in the dumps of Eldorado and Bonanza, and there was but little money to spend. A man with a good claim could get a certain amount of credit, but the bulk of the business was transacted in cash. Money commanded 5 to 10 per cent a month. The commercial companies and the saloons were the custodians of dust. A miner would hand his sack containing perhaps thousands of dollars to a saloonkeeper, who put it in an unlocked drawer, where it was as safe as in a bank outside.

In a new mining-camp the saloon is the center of social life. At Dawson, shut out from the world, under conditions that tried the very souls of men, it was less wonder that men were drawn together into the only public places where a friendly fire burned by day and night, and where, in the dim light of a kerosene lamp, they might see one another's faces. The Yukon saloon was a peculiar institution (I feel that I am describing something that passed away when the horde of newcomers came later). Most of the proprietors were old-timers who had been miners, men of honor and character, respected in a community where a man was valued, not according to his pretensions or position in "society", but in proportion to his manliness and intrinsic worth. Class lines are not drawn sharply in a mining camp, and the freedom from the restraint of society and home makes temptation greater than many can withstand.

Taken as a whole, the experience of a year in the Klondike is such as to search out the flaw in the weak but to strengthen the character of the strong.

Of the half-dozen or more places of amusement and recreation, the most pretentious was the "Opera House," a large log building, with a bar and various gambling lay-outs in the front, and a theatre in the rear, with a stage, boxes at each side, and benches on the floor for the audience. It gave vaudeville performances, lasting several hours each evening, the performers being mostly a troupe who stamped with the rest from Circle City. The price of admission, strange to say, was at the low price of "four bits." or half a dollar, admission being secured, according to the usual Yukon custom, by first purchasing for that sum a drink or a cigar at the bar. At the end of the performance the benches were taken up, and dancing began and continued all night. The receipts of the place were enormous, footing upwards of $22,000 a month. Early on Thanksgiving morning, after an uproarious masquerade ball, the dry building caught fire, and next morning saw only the blackened ruins of Dawson's first theatre. After the burning of the "Opera-House," the talent took to various occupations, most of the women securing work at the one remaining dance-hall, the "M. & M.," generally known as "Pete's Place" within whose hospitable walls on cold nights it cost the 'busted' *Cheechako* nothing to warm himself at the stove, to listen to the music, to look on at the scene of gaiety, and wet his dry throat at the water barrel. A water barrel in a saloon, think of it! Yes, in the old-time Yukon saloon it stood in a corner, or at the end of the bar, and was kept filled with pure cold water at a cost of $10 a barrel, while a tin dipper hung on a nail for the use of all.

"Pete's" was a two-story log building, the upper story being the living- rooms, of the proprietor. One entered from the street, in a whisk of steam that coated the doorjamb with snowy frost, into a low-ceilinged room some thirty by forty feet in dimensions. The bar, a pine counter stained red, with a large mirror and bottles and glasses behind, was on the left hand. A lunch-counter stood on the right, while in the rear, and fenced off by a low wooden railing, but leaving a way clear to the bar, was the space reserved for dancing. Here, in the glow of three or four dim, smoky kerosene lamps, around a great sheet-iron "ram-down" stove, kept always red-hot, would always be found a motley crowd — miners government officials, mounted policemen in uniform, gamblers, both amateur and professional, in 'citified' clothes and boiled shirts, old-timers and new-comers, claim-brokers and men with claims to sell, busted men and millionaires — they elbowed each other, talking and laughing, or silently looking on, all in friendly good-nature.

Pete himself, one of the few saloon-keepers who had not been miners in the 'lower country,' served the drinks behind the bar in

shirt-sleeves, with his round head and bull-dog expression, hair carefully oiled and parted, and dark, curled mustache, smiling, courteous,
and ignorant — a typical "outside" bar-tender.

The orchestra consisted of a piano, violin, and flute, and occupied
chairs on a raised platform in one corner of the dance-floor. The
ladies were never backward in importuning partners for the dance;
but any reluctance upon the part of would-be dancers was overcome
by a young man in shirtsleeves, who in a loud, penetrating voice
would begin to exhort:

"Come on, boys — you can all waltz — let's have a nice, long,
juicy waltz;" and then, when three or four couples had taken the
floor, "Fire away!" he would call to the musicians, and then the fun
began. When the dancers had circled around the room five or six
times the music would stop with a jerk, and the couples, with a pre-
cision derived from long practice, would swing towards the bar, and
push their way through the surging mass of interested lookers-on,
or "rubber-necks," in fur-caps, Mackinaws, and parkas, and line up
in front of the bar.

"What 'll you have, gents — a little whiskey?"

Sacks were tossed out on the bar, Pete pushed in front of each
'gent' a small 'blower,' and the 'gent' poured in some gold-dust,
which Pete took to a large gold-scale at the end of the bar, weighed
out $1, and returned the balance to the sack. The lady received as her
commission on the dance a round, white ivory chip, good for 25
cents.

Hardly had the dancers stopped before the caller-off, 'Eddy,' upon
whose skill in keeping the dances going depended the profits of the
house, began again in his loud voice, coaxing, imploring — " Come
on, boys," or, "Grab a lady, boys,' n' have a nice quadrille." And so it
went on all night, one hundred and twenty-five dances being not
unusual before daylight appeared through the frosted panes. Often
the same men danced and caroused night after night, until their
'pokes,' or gold sacks, grew lean, and then they disappeared up the
gulch again.

Whenever a man started in to dance more than one dance he usually paid for several in advance, receiving what are called "allemande
left" chips. There was a difference of opinion, which I believe has
never been settled, as to when a *Cheechako* is entitled to call himself

an "old-timer." Some say after his first winter in the Yukon; others contend not until after he has bought his first "allemande left" chip.

Some of the women were employed at a salary of $125 a week and commissions on extras such as champagne, which cost those who cared to indulge in that luxury $40 a quart. The majority of women received only the 25 cents commission, but sometimes, if industrious or good-looking, they made $25 or even more a night. The whiskey varied greatly in quality, some being very bad, while the best, by the time it reached the consumer, was apt to be diluted to the last degree.

Whenever whiskey runs short the Yukoner falls back upon a villainous decoction made of sourdough, or dough and brown sugar, or sugar alone, and known as "hootchinoo," or "hooch." The still is made of coal-oil cans, the worm of pieces of India-rubber boot-tops cemented together. This crude still is heated over an ordinary Yukon stove. The liquor obtained is clear white, and is flavored with blueberries or dried peaches, to suit the taste. It must be very bad, for its manufacture is forbidden by law; they say it will drive a man crazy; but there were persons willing to take their oath that the regular whiskey sold over some of the bars was worse than "hooch." A home brewed beer, or ale, was also served, a whiskey glassful costing 50 cents. Cigars were mostly a poor five-cent grade.

An example of the better class of Dawson saloon was the "Pioneer," or "Moose horn," a favorite resort of old-timers. The proprietors, Messrs. Densmore, Spencer & McPhee, were types of the early Yukon pioneer. Frank Densmore, in fact, was among the first who crossed the pass, and he rocked for gold on the bars of the upper Yukon a dozen years before the Klondike was known. I recall the "Pioneer" as a large, comfortable room, with the usual bar on one side, having a massive mirror behind, and several large moose and caribou antlers on the walls, a number of unpainted tables and benches and chairs, the latter always filled with men talking over their pipes, reading much-worn newspapers (six months out of date), a few engaged in games of poker, and nine-tenths "dead broke," but as welcome, apparently, as the most reckless rounder who spilled his dust over the bar. It struck the outsider with wonder, the seeming indifference of the proprietors whether one patronized the bar or not, for what other interpretation can one place on a water-barrel at the end of the bar? Then, too, the "busted" man of today might be the "millionaire" of tomorrow; but the reason lay deeper than that. There were men destined not to have fortunes. Very late at night, when Dawson had turned in for a snatch of sleep, one might see them lying on benches and tables. Homeless, stranded men, half-sick and dependent from day to day on the charity of strangers, and who, but for this welcome bench or table, had no place to lay their heads. Something of the generous spirit of the old Yukon life made these men welcome.

Gambling is a miner's proper amusement, provided he also pays his bills. Every saloon had its gambling layouts. "Black-jack," poker, roulette, and craps were played assiduously, some having a preference for one, some for another, but the favorite game was faro. A crowd might always be found around the faro-table, either keeping track of "cases," or simply looking on at the play. Twenty-five cents was the lowest chip, the white, the reds and blues being respectively $1 and $5. The "dealer," sitting behind the table and turning the cards with mechanical regularity, and the "lookout," who saw that "no bets were overlooked," were paid a salary of $15 to $20 a day, and each faro-table had to win from $50 to $80 every day to make a profit for the house, from which a moral may be deduced as to the wicked- ness of playing faro — on the wrong side of the table. At times the play was very large and correspondingly exciting. A young boy who had sold a rich claim "dropped" $18,000 in the course of thirty-six hours' play. Hundreds of dollars were made or lost on the turn of a card. One day a "dog-puncher," Joe Brand, walked in and threw down his sack on the "high card," saying, "That's good for a hun- dred." He won, and was given an order on the weigher for $100. Holding up the slip, he asked, "Is this good for the drinks?" "It is," was the reply, and he ordered up glasses to the number of two hun- dred, had them filled with whiskey, and then invited every one up to drink. A number in the saloon hung back, whom he vainly sought to make drink. He passed off the refusal with a laugh, saying that it must be pretty mean whiskey when no one would drink it. The balance was placed to his credit for another time.

I saw another man, a well-known character, at a "black-jack" table in a few minutes coolly lose an even $1000, and then just to show he didn't mind, he "ordered up" the whole house, treating every one in the saloon, at half a dollar a head, to whiskey and cigars.

Jake, a little Jew who ran a lunch-counter at "Pete's," was partic-ularly fond of dancing and "craps," a game he doubtless learned when a messenger boy in Philadelphia. After a prosperous day's busi-ness Jake would "stake" a dollar, and if he won a sufficient sum he would spend the night dancing. He was too good a businessman to spend the profits of business dancing, and so we always knew when we saw Jake on the floor that he had been lucky that day at craps.

Naturally a restaurant was a profitable undertaking to a person with a well-filled cache. The articles on the bill of fare were limit-ed in number, uncertain in quantity, but unfailingly high in price. An eating-place, with the high-sounding name of "The Eldorado," stood in a space hardly more than ten feet wide, between two larg-er buildings, and consisted of a room front and back, the front room being supplied with three unpainted spruce tables and rough board stools, and a narrow counter between the door and window, on which stood the gold-scales. In the rear was the kitchen. The rough log walls of this "Delmonico's" of Dawson were plastered with signs, à la Bowery, reading: "Meal, $3.50"; "Porterhouse Steak, $8"; "Sirloin Steak, $5." The meal consisted of a bit of moose meat, or beef, beans, a small dish of stewed apples or peaches, one "helping" of bread and butter, and one cup of tea or coffee. In a tent on the waterfront a man and his wife were said to have accumulated $30,000 as the winter's profits, selling coffee and pies, etc. In the "Dominion" saloon was a lunch-counter kept by a freethinking Jew, who discussed philosophy with his customers as he served out plates of soup at $1 each. At Jake's there hung all winter the following bill of fare, drawn in large black letters on a sheet of Bristol-board:

BILL OF FARE

Sandwiches	$.75 each.
Doughnuts	.75 per order.
Pies	.75 cut.
Turnovers.	.75 per order.
Ginger cake	.75 cut.
Coffee cake	1.00 cut.
Caviar sandwiches	1.00 each.
Sardines	1.00 each

Stewed fruits	.50 per dish.
Canned fruits	1.00 per dish.
Cold meats	1.50 order.
Raw Hamburg steak	2.00 order.
Chocolate or cocoa	.75 cup.
Tea or coffee	.50 cup.

  The card and the printing together cost $15, probably one of the most expensive menu cards in the world. Jake's visible stock seldom consisted, at any one time, of more than a bottle of Worcestershire sauce, a pie, a few tins of sardines, some tins of milk, a pan of beans, and a loaf of bread, which were temptingly displayed on three rude shelves against the hack wall. In April, some oysters came in by dog-team. Jake paid $18 and $20 for several tins holding two dozen oysters — less than a pint. There-after an oyster stew could be had for the modest sum of $15. Another person gave $25 each for two of the same tins. A shrewd Yankee, with a winning smile, started a bakery in the Ladue cabin in the middle of the street and made bread and pies, selling them for $1 each. Later he branched out into a restaurant, and took out a fortune.

  Gold dust is not an economical or convenient currency. Out of every $50 expended in making small purchases, there would be a regular loss of $4 to $6, due partly to the custom of the weigher taking the "turn" of the scale, partly to carelessness, and partly to actual theft. In changing dollars and cents into ounces and penny-weights, it is easy to purposely miscalculate or substitute larger weights. And then the small traders had only the pocket prospector's scales, which often were considerably out of balance. The proprietor of one restaurant told me that although he made it a rule not to take the "turn" of the scale, he invariably found himself several dollars ahead at the end of the day.

  When the miner came to town on business, or on pleasure bent, unless he had a cabin, or friends to take him in, he was obliged to choose between staying up all night in the saloons or going to one of the half-dozen establishments by courtesy designated 'hotels.' Not even a person whose sensibilities had been blunted by a year in the Yukon could abide in one even for one night in comfort or safety. The 'hotel' was a two-story building. On the first floor was the bar, which served for the clerk's desk as well, the rear of the place being the family quarters of the proprietor. Upon payment of $2, always demanded in advance, the clerk, bartender, or proprietor — who was often one and the same person — would lead the way with a candle up a rickety stairs to an upper room, which commonly extended the whole length of the building, with only the rafters overhead. Sometimes this room was divided into small rooms or pens by partitions as high as one's head, with just space for a single cot; or else the interior was filled with tiers of double-decked bunks of rude scantling, accommodating twenty or thirty sleepers. The bedding in each bunk consisted of rough blankets and a very small pillow. There was a nail in the wall to hang one's coat upon (for that was all a person was expected to take off, except his shoes or moccasins), and the landlord left a bit of candle to light the guest to bed. The only ventilation to this upper room was through generous cracks in the floor and a small window at each end, which in cold weather were kept scrupulously shut. When heated to a torrid pitch by a large stove on the lower floor, with every bunk full of unwashed men who have taken off their rubber boots or mukluks, the air of this veritable "bull-pen" before morning was such that no one could be induced to repeat the experience except when confronted with the positive alternative of lying out of doors without protection from the cold. Even worse than the thick, nauseating atmosphere were the vermin with which the blankets were alive, as there was no possible means in winter of getting rid of them short of destruction of the bedding. They are already the bane of the diggings, hardly one of the cabins on the older creeks being free from the unwelcome occupants. Clothes-washing was an expensive item, unless one did it himself. No article was less than 50 cents, and it was by no means a large wash that came to $10. Heavy blankets could not be washed at all. Persons regarded themselves as particularly clean if they changed underwear every two weeks.

The hard life led by the miner in winter often brings on a disease known as "scurvy." It is not the same as ship scurvy, and the symptoms vary in different persons, the more common being a hardening of the tendons, especially those under the knee, a darkening of the skin, and an apparent lifelessness of the tissue, so that when a finger is pressed against the skin a dent remains for some time afterwards. It is rarely fatal, though it may incapacitate the victim for work for a whole season. It yields readily to a treatment of spruce-leaf tea, taken internally. Various specific causes are given, such as lack of fresh meat and vegetables, improperly cooked food, exposure and vitiated air, but physicians say that the real cause is yet unknown. Physicians did uncommonly well. The charge for a visit in town was never less than $5, while a visit to the mines was sometimes as high as $500, the charge being regulated according to the "victim's" ability to pay; and the price of drugs was proportionately high. One young doctor was said to have earned $1200 to $1500 a month, while another who invested his earnings judiciously in mines was reputed to have made $200,000. The hospital, although a sectarian institution, was maintained by local subscriptions. Three ounces of gold-dust ($51) entitled a person to a ticket for treatment during one year, and a certain number of weeks in the hospital, with board and nursing free. To non-subscribers the charge was $5 a day, and $5 extra for the doctor's usually daily visit. From its establishment in the fall of 1897 up to April 1st, 1898, the number of deaths was twenty-four, of which seven or eight were from typhoid fever. The hospital was a godsend, and many a man came out from under the tender care of the venerable Father Judge and the little band of Sisters with a broader view of religious work and a better personal understanding of what it meant to devote one's life to doing good for his fellowmen.

The One Thousand Dozen
Jack London

David Rasmunsen was a hustler, and, like many a greater man, a man of the one idea. Wherefore, when the clarion call of the North rang on his ear, he conceived an adventure in eggs and bent all his energy to its achievement. He figured briefly and to the point, and the adventure became iridescent-hued, splendid. That eggs would sell at Dawson for five dollars a dozen was a safe working premise. Whence it was incontrovertible that one thousand dozen would bring, in the Golden Metropolis, five thousand dollars.

On the other hand, expense was to be considered, and he considered it well, for he was a careful man, keenly practical, with a hard head and a heart that imagination never warmed. At fifteen cents a dozen, the initial cost of his thousand dozen would be one hundred and fifty dollars, a mere bagatelle in face of the enormous profit. And suppose, just suppose, to be wildly extravagant for once, that transportation for himself and eggs should run up eight hundred and fifty more; he would still have four thousand clear cash and clean when the last egg was disposed of and the last dust had rippled into his sack.

"You see, Alma" — he figured it over with his wife, the cozy dining room submerged in a sea of maps, government surveys, guidebooks, and Alaskan itineraries — "you see, expenses don't really begin till you make Dyea — fifty dollars'll cover it with a first-class passage thrown in. Now from Dyea to Lake Lindeman, Indian packers take your goods over for twelve cents a pound, twelve dollars a hundred, or one hundred and twenty dollars a thousand. Say I have fifteen hundred pounds, it'll cost one hundred and eighty dollars — call it two hundred to be safe. I am creditably informed by a Klondiker just come out that I can buy a boat for three hundred. But the same man say's I'm sure to get a couple of passengers for one hundred and fifty each, which will give me the boat for nothing, and, further, they can help me manage it. And... that's all; I put my eggs ashore from the boat at Dawson. Now let me see, how much is that?"

"Fifty dollars from San Francisco to Dyea, two hundred from Dyea to Lindeman, passengers pay for the boat — two hundred and fifty all told," she summed up swiftly, went on happily; "that leaves a margin of five hundred for emergencies. And what possible emergencies can arise?"

Alma shrugged her shoulders and elevated her brows. If that vast Northland was capable of swallowing up a man and a thousand dozen eggs, surely there was room and to spare for whatever else he might happen to possess. So she thought, but she said nothing. She knew David Rasmunsen too well to say anything.

"Doubling the time because of chance delays, I should make the trip in two months. Think of it, Alma! Four thousand in two months! Beats the paltry hundred a month I'm getting now. Why, we'll build further out where we'll have more space, gas in every room, and a view, and the rent of the cottage'll pay taxes, insurance, and water, and leave something over. And then there's always the chance of my striking it and coming out a millionaire. Now tell me, Alma, don't you think I'm very moderate?"

And Alma could hardly think otherwise. Besides, had not her own cousin — though a remote and distant one to be sure, the black sheep, the harum-scarum, the ne'er-do-well — had not he come down out of that weird North country with a hundred thousand in yellow dust, to say nothing of a half-ownership in the hole from which it came?

David Rasmunsen's grocer was surprised when he found him weighing eggs in the scales at the end of the counter, and Rasmunsen himself was more surprised when he found that a dozen eggs weighed a pound and a half — fifteen hundred pounds for his thousand dozen! There would be no weight left for his clothes, blankets, and cooking utensils, to say nothing of the grub he must necessarily consume by the way. His calculations were all thrown out, and he was just proceeding to recast them when he hit upon the idea of weighing small eggs. "For whether they be large or small, a dozen eggs is a dozen eggs," he observed sagely to himself; and a dozen small ones he found to weigh but a pound and a quarter. The city of San Francisco was overrun by anxious-eyed emissaries, and commission houses and dairy associations were startled by a sudden demand for eggs running not more than twenty ounces to the dozen.

Rasmunsen mortgaged the little cottage for a thousand dollars, arranged for his wife to make a prolonged stay among her own people, threw up his job, and started north. To keep within his schedule he compromised on a second-class passage, which, because of the rush, was worse than steerage; and in the late summer, a pale and wobbly man, he disembarked with his eggs on the Dyea beach. But it did not take him long to recover his land legs and appetite. His first interview with the Chilkoot packers straightened him up and stiffened his backbone. Forty cents a pound they demanded for the twenty-eight-mile portage, and while he caught his breath and swallowed, the price went up to forty-three. Fifteen husky Indians put the straps on his packs at forty-five, but took them off at an offer of forty-seven from a Skagway Croesus in dirty shirt and ragged overalls who had lost his horses on the White Pass Trail and was now making a last desperate drive at the country by way of Chilkoot.

But Rasmunsen was clean grit, and at fifty cents found takers, who, two days later, set his eggs down intact at Lindeman. But fifty cents a pound is a thousand dollars a ton, and his fifteen hundred pounds had exhausted his emergency fund and left him stranded at the Tantalus point where each day he saw the fresh-ship sawed boats departing for Dawson. Further, a great anxiety brooded over the camp where the boats were built. Men worked frantically, early and late, at the height of their endurance, calking, nailing and pitching in a frenzy of haste for which adequate explanation was not far to seek. Each day the snow-line crept farther down the bleak, rock-shouldered peaks, and gale followed gale, with sleet and slush and snow, and in the eddies and quiet places young ice formed and thickened through the fleeting hours. And each morn, toil-stiffened men turned wan faces across the lake to see if the freeze-up had come. For the freeze-up heralded the death of their hope — the hope that they would be floating down the swift river ere navigation closed on the chain of lakes.

To harrow Rasmunsen's soul further, he discovered three competitors in the egg business. It was true that one, a little German, had gone broke and was himself forlornly back tripping the last pack of the portage; but the other two had boats nearly completed and were daily supplicating the god of merchants and traders to stay the iron hand of winter for just another day. But the iron hand closed down over the land. Men were being frozen in the blizzard, which swept Chilkoot, and Rasmunsen frosted his toes before he was aware. He found a chance to go passenger with his freight in a boat just shoving off through the rubble, but two hundred, hard cash, was required, and he had no money.

"Ay tank you yust wait one leedle w'ile," said the Swedish boatbuilder, who had struck his Klondike right there and was wise enough to know it — "one leedle w'ile and I make you a tam fine skiff boat, sure Pete."

With this unpledged word to go on, Rasmunsen hit the back trail to Crater Lake, where he fell in with two press correspondents whose tangled baggage was strewn from Stone House, over across the Pass, and as far as Happy Camp.

"Yes," he said with consequence. "I've a thousand dozen eggs at Lindeman, and my boat's just about got the last seam calked. Consider myself in luck to get it. Boats are at a premium, you know, and none to be had."

Whereupon and almost with bodily violence the correspondents clamored to go with him, fluttered greenbacks before his eyes, and spilled yellow twenties from hand to hand. He could not hear of it, but they overpersuaded him, and he reluctantly consented to take them at three hundred apiece. Also they pressed upon him the passage money in advance. And while they wrote to their respective journals concerning the Good Samaritan with the thousand dozen eggs, the Good Samaritan was hurrying back to the Swede at Lindeman.

"Here, you! Gimme that boat!" was his salutation, his hand jingling the correspondents' gold pieces and his eyes hungrily bent upon the finished craft.

The Swede regarded him stolidly and shook his head.

"How much is the other fellow paying? Three hundred? Well, here's four. Take it."

He tried to press it upon him, but the man backed away. "Ay tank not. Ay say him get der skiff boat. You just wait —"

"Here's six hundred. Last call. Take it or leave it. Tell'm it's a mistake."

The Swede wavered. "Ay tank yes," he finally said, the last Rasmunsen saw of him his vocabulary was going to wreck in a vain effort to explain the mistake to the other fellow.

The German slipped and broke his ankle on the steep hog back above Deer Lake, sold out his stock for a dollar a dozen, and with the proceeds hired Indian packers to carry him back to Dyea. But on the morning Rasmunsen shoved off with his correspondents, his two rivals followed suit.

"How many you got?" one of them, a lean little New Englander, called out.

"One thousand dozen," Rasmunsen answered proudly.

"Huh! I'll go you even stakes I beat you in with my eight hundred."

The correspondents offered to lend him the money; but Rasmunsen declined, and the Yankee closed with the remaining rival, a brawny son of the sea and sailor of ships and things, who promised to show them all a wrinkle or two when it came to cracking on. And crack on he did, with a large tarpaulin square sail which pressed the bow half under at every jump. He was the first to run out of Lindeman, but, disdaining the portage, piled his loaded boat on the rocks in the boiling rapids. Rasmunsen and the Yankee, who likewise had two passengers, portaged across on their backs and then lined their empty boats down through the bad water to Bennett.

Bennett was a twenty-five-mile lake, narrow and deep, a funnel between the mountains through which storms ever romped. Rasmunsen camped on the sandpit at its head, where were many men and boats bound north in the teeth of the Arctic winter. He awoke in the morning to find a piping gale from the south, which caught the chill from the whited peaks and glacial valleys and blew as cold as north wind ever blew. But it was fair, and he also found the Yankee staggering past the first bold headland with all sail set. Boat after boat was getting under way, and the correspondents fell to with enthusiasm.

"We'll catch him before Caribou Crossing," they assured Rasmunsen, as they ran up the sail and the *Alma* took the first icy spray over her bow.

Now Rasmunsen all his life had been prone to cowardice on water, but he clung to the kicking steering-oar with set face and determined jaw. His thousand dozen were there in the boat before his eyes, safely secured beneath the correspondents' baggage, and somehow, before his eyes, were the little cottage and the mortgage for a thousand dollars.

It was bitter cold. Now and again he hauled in the steering sweep and put out a fresh one while his passengers chopped the ice from the blade. Wherever the spray struck, it turned instantly to frost, and the dipping boom of the spritsail was quickly fringed with icicles. The *Alma* strained and hammered through the big seas till the seams and butts began to spread, but in lieu of bailing the correspondents chopped ice and flung it overboard. There was no let-up. The mad race with winter was on, and the boats tore along in a desperate string.

"W-w-we can't stop to save our souls!" one of the correspondents chattered, from cold, not fright.

"That's right! Keep her down the middle, old man!" the other encouraged.

Rasmunsen replied with an idiotic grin. The ironbound shores were in a lather of foam, and even down the middle the only hope was to keep running away from the big seas. To lower sail was to be overtaken and swamped. Time and again they passed boats pounding among the rocks, and once they saw one on the edge of the breakers about to strike. A little craft behind them, with two men, jibed over and turned bottom up.

"W-w-watch out, old man!" cried he of the chattering teeth.

Rasmunsen grinned and tightened his aching grip on the sweep. Scores of times had the send of the sea caught the big square stern of the *Alma* and thrown her off from dead before it, till the after leach of the spritsail fluttered hollowly, and each time, and only with all his strength, had he forced her back. His grin by then had become fixed, and it disturbed the correspondents to look at him.

They roared down past an isolated rock a hundred yards from shore. From its wave-drenched top a man shrieked wildly, for the instant cutting the storm with his voice. But the next instant the *Alma* was by, and the rock growing a black speck in the troubled froth.

"That settles the Yankee! Where's the sailor?" shouted one of his passengers.

Rasmunsen shot a glance over his shoulder at the black square sail. He had seen it leap up out of the gray to windward, and for an hour, off and on, had been watching it grow. The sailor had evidently repaired damages and was making up for lost time.

"Look at him come!"

Both passengers stopped chopping ice to watch. Twenty miles of Bennett were behind them — room and to spare for the sea to toss up its mountains toward the sky. Sinking and soaring like a storm god, the sailor drove by them. The huge sail seemed to grip the boat from the crests of the waves, to tear it bodily out of the water, and fling it crashing and smothering down into the yawning troughs.

"The sea'll never catch him!"

"But he'll r-r-run her nose under!"

Even as they spoke, the black tarpaulin swooped from sight behind a big comber. The next wave rolled over the spot, and the next, but the boat did not reappear. The *Alma* rushed by the place. A little riffraff of cars and boxes was seen. An arm thrust up and a shaggy head broke surface a score of yards away.

For a time there was silence. As the end of the lake came in sight, the waves began to leap aboard with such steady recurrence that the correspondents no longer chopped ice but flung the water out with buckets. Even this would not do, and, after a shouted conference with Rasmunsen, they attacked the baggage. Flour, bacon, beans, blankets, cooking stoves, ropes, odds and ends, everything they could get hands on, flew overboard. The boat acknowledged it at once, taking less water and rising more buoyantly.

"That'll do!" Rasmunsen called sternly, as they applied themselves to the top layer of eggs.

"The h-hell it will!" answered the shivering one, savagely. With the exception of their notes, films, and cameras, they had sacrificed their outfit. He bent over, laid hold of an egg-box, and began to worry it out from under the lashing.

"Drop it! Drop it, I say!"

Rasmunsen had managed to draw his revolver, and with the crook of his arm over the sweep head was taking aim. The correspondent stood up on the thwart, balancing back and forth, his face twisted with menace and speechless anger.

"My God!"

So cried his brother correspondent, hurling himself, face downward, into the bottom of the boat. The *Alma*, under the divided attention of Rasmunsen, had been caught by a great mass of water and whirled around. The after leach hollowed, the sail emptied and jibed, and the boom, sweeping with terrific force across the boat, carried the angry correspondent overboard with a broken back. Mast and sail had gone over the side as well. A drenching sea followed, as the boat lost headway, and Rasmunsen sprang to the bailing bucket.

Several boats hurtled past them in the next half-hour — small boats, boats of their own size, boats afraid, unable to do aught but run madly on. Then a ten-ton barge, at imminent risk of destruction, lowered sail to windward and lumbered down upon them.

"Keep off! Keep off!" Rasmunsen screamed.

But his low gunwale ground against the heavy craft, and the remaining correspondent clambered aboard. Rasmunsen was over the eggs like a cat and in the bow of the *Alma*, striving with numb fingers to bend the hauling-lines together.

"Come on!" a red-whiskered man yelled at him.

"I've a thousand dozen eggs here," he shouted back. "Gimme a tow! I'll pay you!"

"Come on!" they howled in chorus.

A big whitecap broke just beyond, washing over the barge and leaving the *Alma* half swamped. The men cast off, cursing him as they ran up their sail. Rasmunsen cursed back and fell to bailing. The mast and sail, like a sea anchor, still fast by the halyards, held the boat head on to wind and sea and gave him a chance to fight the water out.

Three hours later, numbed, exhausted, blathering like a lunatic, but still bailing, he went ashore on an ice-strewn beach near Caribou Crossing. Two men, a government courier and a half-breed voyageur, dragged him out of the under surf, saved his cargo, and beached the *Alma*. They were paddling out of the country in a Peterborough, and gave him shelter for the night in their storm-bound camp. Next morning they departed, but he elected to stay by his eggs. And thereafter the name and fame of the man with the thousand dozen eggs began to spread through the land. Gold-seekers who made in before the freeze-up carried the news of his coming. Grizzled old-timers of Forty Mile and Circle City, sourdoughs with leathern jaws and bean-calloused stomachs, called up dream memories of chickens and green things at mention of his name. Dyea and Skagway took an interest in his being, and questioned his progress from every man who came over the passes, while Dawson — golden, omelet less Dawson — fretted and worried, and waylaid every chance arrival for word of him.

But of this, Rasmunsen knew nothing. The day after the wreck he patched up the *Alma* and pulled out. A cruel east wind blew in his teeth from Tagish, but he got the oars over the side and bucked manfully into it, though half the time he was drifting backward and chopping ice from the blades. According to the custom of the country, he was driven ashore at Windy Arm; three times on Tagish saw him swamped and beached; and Lake Marsh held him at the freeze-up. The *Alma* was crushed in the jamming of the floes, but the eggs were intact. These he back-tripped two miles across the ice to the shore, where he built a cache, which stood for years after and was pointed out by men who knew.

Half a thousand frozen miles stretched between him and Dawson, and the waterway was closed. But Rasmunsen, with a peculiar tense look in his face, struck back up the lakes on foot. What he suffered on that lone trip, with naught but a single blanket, an axe, and a handful of beans, is not given to ordinary mortals to know. Only the Arctic adventurer may understand. Suffice that he was caught in a blizzard on Chilkoot and left two of his toes with the surgeon at Sheep Camp. Yet he stood on his feet and washed dishes in the scullery of the *Pawona* to the Puget Sound, and from here passed coal on a P. S. boat to San Francisco.

It was a haggard, unkempt man who limped across the shining office floor to raise a second mortgage from the bank people. His hollow cheeks betrayed themselves through the scraggly beard, and his eyes seemed to have retired into deep caverns where they burned with cold fires. His hands were grained from exposure and hard work, and the nails were rimmed with tight-packet dirt and coal dust. He spoke vaguely of eggs and ice-packs, winds and tides; but when they declined to let him have more than a second thousand, his talk became incoherent, concerning itself chiefly with the price of dogs and dog-food, and such things as snowshoes and moccasins and winter trails. They let him have fifteen hundred, which was more than the cottage warranted, and breathed easier when he scrawled his signature and passed out the door.

Two weeks later he went over Chilkoot with three dog sleds of five dogs each. One team he drove, the two Indians with him driving the others. At Lake Marsh they broke out the cache and loaded up. But there was no trail. He was the first in over the ice, and to him fell the task of packing the snow and hammering away through the rough river jams. Behind him he often observed a campfire smoke trickling thinly up through the quiet air, and he wondered why the people did not overtake him. For he was a stranger to the land and did not understand. Nor could he understand his Indians when they tried to explain. This they conceived to be a hardship, but when they balked and refused to break camp of mornings, he drove them to their work at pistol point.

When he slipped through an ice bridge near the White Horse and froze his foot, tender yet and oversensitive from the previous freezing, the Indians looked for him to lie up. But he sacrificed a blanket, and, with his foot encased in an enormous moccasin, big as a water-bucket, continued to take his regular turn with the front sled. Here was the cruelest work, and they respected him, though on the side they rapped their foreheads with their knuckles and significantly shook their heads. One night they tried to run away, but the zip-zip of his bullets in the snow brought them back, snarling but convinced. Whereupon, being only savage Chilkat men, they put their heads together to kill him; but he slept like a cat, and, waking or sleeping, the chance never came. Often they tried to tell him the import of the smoke wreath in the rear, but he could not comprehend and grew suspicious of them. And when they sulked or shirked, he was quick to let drive at them between the eyes, and quick to cool their heated souls with sight of his ready revolver.

And so it went — with mutinous men, wild dogs, and a trail that broke the heart. He fought the men to stay with him, fought the dogs to keep them away from the eggs, fought the ice, the cold, and the pain of his foot, which would not heal. As fast as the young tissue renewed, it was bitten and seared by the frost, so that a running sore developed, into which he could almost shove his fist. In the mornings, when he first put his weight upon it, his head went dizzy, and he was near to fainting from the pain; but later on in the day it usually grew numb, to recommence when he crawled into his blankets and tried to sleep. Yet he, who had been a clerk and sat at a desk all his days, toiled till the Indians were exhausted, and even outworked the dogs. How hard he worked, how much he suffered, he did not know. Being a man of the one idea, now that the idea had come, it mastered him. In the foreground of his consciousness was Dawson, in the background his thousand dozen eggs, and midway between the two his ego fluttered, striving always to draw them together to a glittering golden point. This golden point was the five thousand dollars, the consummation of the idea and the point of departure for whatever new idea might present itself. For the rest, he was a mere automaton. He was unaware of other things, seeing them as through a glass darkly, and giving them no thought. The work of his hands he did with machine-like wisdom; likewise the work of his head. So the look on his face grew very tense, till even the Indians were afraid of it, was and marveled at the strange white man who had made them slaves and forced them to toil with such foolishness.

There came a snap on Lake Laberge, when the cold of outer space smote the tip of the planet, and the frost ranged sixty and odd degrees below zero. Here, laboring with open mouth that he might breathe more freely, he chilled his lungs, and for the rest of the trip he was troubled with a dry, hacking cough, especially irritable in smoke of camp or under stress of undue exertion. On the Thirty Mile River he found much open water, spanned by precarious ice bridges and fringed with narrow rim ice, tricky and uncertain. The rim ice was impossible to reckon on, and he dared it without reckoning, falling back on his revolver when his drivers demurred. But on the ice bridges, covered with snow though they were, precautions could be taken. These they crossed on their snowshoes, with long poles, held crosswise in their hands, to which to cling in case of accident. Once over, the dogs were called to follow. And on such a bridge, where the absence of the center ice was masked by the snow, one of the Indians met his end. He went through as quickly and neatly as a knife through thin cream, and the current swept him from view down under the stream ice.

That night his mate fled away through the pale moonlight, Rasmunsen futilely puncturing the silence with his revolver — a thing he handled with more celerity than cleverness. Thirty-six hours later the Indian made a police camp on the five Big Salmon. "Um-um-um funny mans — what you call? — top um head all loose," the interpreter explained to the puzzled captain. "Eh? Yet, clazy, much clazy mans. Eggs, eggs, all a time eggs — savvy? Come bime-by."

It was several days before Rasmunsen arrived, the three sleds lashed together, and all the dogs in a single team. It was awkward, and where the going was bad he was compelled to back-trip it sled by sled, though he managed most of the time, through Herculean efforts, to bring all along on the one haul. He did not seem moved when the captain of police told him his man was hitting the high places for Dawson, and was by that time, probably, halfway between Selkirk and Stewart. Nor did he appear interested when informed that the police had broken the trail as far as Pelly; for he had attained to a fatalistic acceptance of all natural dispensations, good or ill. But when they told him that Dawson was in the bitter clutch of famine, he smiled, threw the harness on his dogs, and pulled out.

But it was at his next halt that the mystery of the smoke was explained. With the word at Big Salmon that the trail was broken to Pelly, there was no longer any need for the smoke wreath to linger in his wake; and Rasmunsen, crouching over his lonely fire, saw a motley string of sleds go by. First came the courier and the half-breed who had hauled him out from Bennett; then mail-carriers for Circle City, two sleds of them, and a mixed following of ingoing Klondikers. Dogs and men were fresh and fat, while Rasmunsen and his brutes were jaded and worn down to the skin and bone. They of the smoke wreath had traveled one day in three, resting and reserving their strength for the dash to come when broken trail was met with; while each day he had plunged and floundered forward, breaking the spirit of his dogs and robbing them of their mettle.

As for himself, he was unbreakable. They thanked him kindly for his efforts in their behalf, those fat, fresh men — thanked him kindly, with broad grins and ribald laughter; and now, when he understood, he made no answer. Nor did he cherish silent bitterness. It was immaterial. The idea — the fact behind the idea — was not changed. Here he was and his thousand dozen; there was Dawson; the problem was unaltered.

At the Little Salmon, being short of dog food, the dogs got into his grub, and from there to Selkirk, he lived on beans — coarse, brown beans, big beans, grossly nutritive, which griped his stomach and doubled him up at two-hour intervals. But the Factor at Selkirk had a notice on the door of the Post to the effect that no steamer had been up the Yukon for two years, and in consequence grub was beyond price. He offered to swap flour, however, at the rate of a cupful for each egg, but Rasmunsen shook his head and hit the trail. Below the Post he managed to buy frozen horsehide for the dogs, the horses having been slain by the Chilkat cattlemen, and the scraps and offal preserved by the Indians. He tackled the hide himself, but the hair worked into the bean sores of his mouth, and was beyond endurance.

Here at Selkirk, he met the forerunners of the hungry exodus of Dawson, and from there on they crept over the trail, a dismal throng. "No grub!" was the song they sang. "No grub, and had to go." "Everybody holding candles for a rise in the spring." "Flour dollar'n a half a pound, and no sellers."

"Eggs?" one of them answered. "Dollar apiece, but they ain't none."

Rasmunsen made a rapid calculation. "Twelve thousand dollars," he said aloud.

"Hye?" the man asked.

"Nothing," he answered, and mushed the dogs along.

When he arrived at Stewart River, seventy miles from Dawson, five of his dogs were gone, and the remainder were falling in the traces, hauling with what little strength was left in them. Even then he was barely crawling along ten miles a day. His cheekbones and nose, frost-bitten again and again, were turned bloody black and hideous. The thumb, which was separated from the fingers by the gee-pole, had likewise been nipped and gave him great pain. The monstrous moccasin still encased his foot, and strange pains were beginning to rack the leg. At Sixty Mile, the last beans, which he had been rationing for some time, were finished; yet he steadfastly refused to touch the eggs. He could not reconcile his mind to the legitimacy of it, and staggered and fell along the way to Indian River. Here a fresh-killed moose and an open-handed old-timer gave him and his dogs new strength, and at Ainslie's he felt repaid for it all when a stampeder, ripe from Dawson in five hours, was sure he could get a dollar and a quarter for every egg he possessed.

He came up the steep bank by the Dawson barracks with fluttering heart and shaking knees. The dogs were so weak that he was forced to rest them, and, waiting, he leaned limply against the gee-pole. A man, an eminently decorous-looking man, came sauntering by in a great bearskin coat. He glanced at Rasmunsen curiously, then stopped and ran for a speculative eye over the dogs and the three lashed sleds.

"What you got?" he asked.

"Eggs," Rasmunsen answered huskily, hardly able to pitch his voice above a whisper.

"Eggs! Whoopee! Whoopee!" He sprang up into the air, gyrated madly, and finished with half a dozen war steps. "You don't say—all of 'em?"

"All of 'em?"

"Say, you must be the Egg Man." He walked around and viewed Rasmunsen from the other side. "Come, now, ain't you the Egg Man?"

Rasmunsen didn't know, but supposed he was, and the man sobered down a bit.

"What d'ye expect to get for 'em?" he asked cautiously.

Rasmunsen became audacious. "Dollar'n a half," he said.

"Done!" the man came back promptly. "Gimme a dozen."

"I — I mean a dollar'n a half apiece," Rasmunsen hesitatingly explained.

"Sure. I heard you. Make it two dozen. Here's the dust." The man pulled out a healthy gold sack the size of a small sausage and knocked it negligently against the gee-pole. Rasmunsen felt a strange trembling in the pit of his stomach, a tickling of the nostrils, and an almost overwhelming desire to sit down and cry. But a curious, wide-eyed crowd was beginning to collect, and man after man was calling out for eggs. He was without scales, but the man with the bearskin coat fetched a pair and obligingly weighed in the dust while Rasmunsen passed out the goods. Soon there was a pushing and shoving and shouldering, and a great clamor. Everybody wanted to buy and to be served first. And as the excitement grew, Rasmunsen cooled down. This would never do. There must be something behind the fact of their buying so eagerly. It would be wiser if he rested first and sized up the market. Perhaps eggs were worth two dollars apiece. Anyway, whenever he wished to sell, he was sure of a dollar and a half. "Stop!" he cried, when a couple of hundred had been sold. "No more now. I'm played out. I've got to get a cabin, and then you can come and see me."

A groan went up at this, but the man with the bearskin coat approved. Twenty-four of the frozen eggs went rattling in his capacious pockets and he didn't care whether the rest of the town ate or not. Besides, he could see Rasmunsen was on his last legs.

"There's a cabin right around the second corner from the Monte Carlo," he told him — "the one with the sody-bottle window. It ain't mine, but I've got charge of it. Rents for ten a day and cheap for the money. You move right in, and I'll see you later. Don't forget the sody-bottle window."

"Tra-la-loo!" he called back a moment later. "I'm goin' up the hill to eat eggs and dream of home."

On his way to the cabin, Rasmunsen recollected he was hungry and bought a small supply of provisions at the N.A.T. & T. store — also a beefsteak at the butcher shop and dried salmon for the dogs. He found the cabin without difficulty and left the dogs in the harness while he started the fire and got the coffee under way.

"A dollar'n a half apiece — one thousand dozen — eighteen thousand dollars!" He kept muttering it to himself, over and over, as he went about his work.

As he flopped the steak into the frying pan the door opened. He turned. It was the man with the bearskin coat. He seemed to come in with determination, as though bound on some explicit errand, but as he looked at Rasmunsen an expression of perplexity came into his face.

"I say — now I say — " he began, then halted.

Rasmunsen wondered if he wanted the rent.

"I say, damn it, you know, them eggs is bad."

Rasmunsen staggered. He felt as though some one had struck him an astounding blow between the eyes. The walls of the cabin reeled and tilted up. He put out his hand to steady himself and rested it on the stove. The sharp pain and the smell of the burning flesh brought him back to himself.

"I see," he said slowly, fumbling in his pocket for the sack. "You want your money back."

"It ain't the money," the man said, "but hain't you got any eggs — good?"

Rasmunsen shook his head. "You'd better take the money."

But the man refused and backed way. "I'll come back," he said, "when you've taken stock, and get what's comin'."

Rasmunsen rolled the chopping block into the cabin and carried in the eggs. He went about it quite calmly. He took up the hand-axe, and, one by one, chopped the eggs in half. These halves he examined carefully and let fall to the floor. At first he sampled from the different cases, then deliberately emptied one case at a time. The heap on the floor grew larger. The coffee boiled over and the smoke of the burning beefsteak filled the cabin. He chopped steadfastly and monotonously till the last case was finished.

Somebody knocked at the door, knocked again, and let himself in. "What a mess!" he remarked, as he paused and surveyed the scene. The severed eggs were beginning to thaw in the heat of the stove, and a miserable odor was growing stronger.

"Must a-happened on the steamer," he suggested.

Rasmunsen looked at him long and blankly.

"I'm Murray, Big Jim Murray, everybody knows me," the man volunteered. "I'm just hearin' your eggs is rotten, and I'm offerin' you two hundred for the batch. They ain't good as salmon, but still they're fair scoffin's for dogs."

Rasmunsen seemed turned to stone. He did not move. "You go to hell," he said passionlessly.

"Now just consider. I pride myself it's a decent price for a mess like that, and it's better'n nothin'. Two hundred. What you say?"

"You go to hell," Rasmunsen repeated softly, "and get out of here." Murray gaped with a great awe, then went out carefully, backward, with his eyes fixed on the other's face.

Rasmunsen followed him out and turned the dogs loose. He threw them all the salmon he had bought, and coiled a sled lashing up in his hand. Then he reentered the cabin and drew the latch in after him. The smoke from the cindered steak made his eyes smart. He stood on the bunk, passed the lashing over the ridgepole, and measured the swing-off with his eye. It did not seem to satisfy, for he put the stool on the bunk and climbed upon the stool. He drove a noose in the end of the lashing and slipped his head through. The other end he made fast. Then he kicked the stool out from under.

The Shooting of Dan McGrew
Robert Service

A Bunch of the boys were whooping it up
   in the Malamute saloon;
The kid that handles the music-box
   was hitting a jag-time tune;
Back of the bar, in a solo game,
   sat Dangerous Dan McGrew,
And watching his luck was his light-o'-love,
   the lady that's known as Lou.

When out of the night, which was fifty below,
   and into the din and the glare,
There stumbled a miner fresh from the creeks,
   dog-dirty, and loaded for bear.
He looked like a man with a foot in the grave
   and scarcely the strength of a louse,
Yet he tilted a poke of dust on the bar,
   and he called for drinks for the house.
There was none could place the stranger's face,
   though we searched ourselves for a clue;
But we drank his health, and the last to drink
   was Dangerous Dan McGrew.

There's men that somehow just grip your eyes,
   and hold them hard like a spell;
And such was he, and he looked to me
   like a man who had lived in hell;
With a face most hair, and the dreary stare
   of a dog whose day is done,
As he watered the green stuff in his glass,
   and the drops fell one by one.
Then I got to figgering who he was,

and wondering what he'd do,
And I turned my head — and there watching him
   was the lady that's known as Lou.

His eyes went rubbering round the room,
   and he seemed in a kind of daze,
Till at last that old piano fell
   in the way of his wandering gaze.
The ragtime kid was having a drink;
   there was no one else on the stool,
So the stranger stumbles across the room,
   and flops down there like a fool.
In a buckskin shirt that was glazed with dirt
   he sat, and I saw him sway;
Then he clutched the keys with his talon hands
   — my God, but that man could play!

Were you ever out in the Great Alone,
   when the moon was awful clear,
And the icy mountains hemmed you in
   with a silence you most could hear;
With only the howl of a timber wolf,
   and you camped there in the cold,
A half-dead thing in a stark, dead world,
   clean mad for the muck called gold;
While high overhead, green, yellow, and red,
   the North Lights swept in bars? —
Then you've a hunch what the music meant...
   hunger and night and the stars.

And hunger not of the belly kind
   that's banished with bacon and beans,
But the gnawing hunger of lonely men
   for a home and all that it means;
For a fireside far from the cares that are,

four walls and a roof above;
But oh! so cramful of cozy joy,
   and crowned with a woman's love —
A woman dearer than all the world,
   and true as Heaven is true...
(God! how ghastly she looks through her rouge —
the lady that's known as Lou.)

Then on a sudden the music changed,
   so soft that you scarce could hear;
But you felt that your life had been looted clean
   of all that it once held dear;
That someone had stolen the woman you loved;
   that her love was a devil's lie;
That your guts were gone, and the best for you
   was to crawl away and die.
'Twas the crowning cry of a heart's despair,
   and it thrilled you through and through —
"I guess I'll make it a spread misère,"
   said Dangerous Dan McGrew.

The music almost died away...
   then it burst like a pent-up flood;
And it seemed to say, "Repay, repay,"
   and my eyes were blind with blood.
The thought came back of an ancient wrong,
   and it stung like a frozen lash,
And the lust awoke to kill, to kill...
   then the music stopped with a crash,
And the stranger turned, and his eyes they burned
   in a most peculiar way;
In a buckskin shirt that was glazed with dirt
   he sat, and I saw him sway;
Then his lips went in in a kind of grin,
   and he spoke, and his voice was calm,
And "Boys," says he, "you don't know me,

and none of you care a damn;
But I want to state, and my words are straight,
   and I'll bet my poke they're true,
That one of you is a hound of hell…
   and that one is Dan McGrew."

Then I ducked my head, and the lights went out,
   and two guns blazed in the dark,
And a woman screamed, and the lights went up,
   and two men lay stiff and stark.
Pitched on his head, and pumped full of lead,
   was Dangerous Dan McGrew,
While the man from the creeks lay clutched
   to the breast of the lady that's known as Lou.

These are the simple facts of the case,
   and I guess I ought to know.
They say that the stranger was crazed with "hooch,"
   and I'm not denying it's so.
I'm not so wise as the lawyer guys,
   but strictly between us two —
The woman that kissed him — and pinched his poke —
   was the lady that's known as Lou.

Exodus

During the late summer of 1899, rumors were circulating of a gold strike at Nome, Alaska. Almost overnight the idle stampeders in Dawson City packed their raggedy belongings and started down the Yukon River to Nome. Sternwheelers were oversold as stampeders raced to the new bonanza. Most would leave Nome a few months later, even poorer than when they left Dawson City. After Nome there would be small strikes on the Yentna, Susitna and Tanana rivers, but none would come close to the size and scale of the Klondike. A handful of stampeders would follow these echo booms for the rest of their lives without finding any riches.

By the autumn of 1899, Dawson City was relatively deserted. Gold was still being mined, but large companies began buying claims from the small independent miners. Enormous dredges replaced the rocker boxes and sluices. The dredges were less labor-intensive and those who worked them were employees, not owner operators. The Klondike Gold Rush was over.

The vast majority of the stampeders left the Yukon without making a cent. They had experienced one of the most arduous treks imaginable. The stampeders had traveled up the coast in overcrowded and often decrepit ships. They had spent the winter ferrying supplies over the cold and dangerous Chilkoot Pass and had built rickety boats and navigated the lakes and rapids of the Yukon River system. Returning home would present many challenges, but these would pale in comparison to what they had endured. They had experienced the adventure of a lifetime.

The North would never be the same. A pattern of development had been established which meant great changes for Indians, settlers and the natural environment. These changes had their benefits and their costs. The Klondike Gold Rush had effects which are still felt to this day.

Exodus
William B. Haskell

During the summer and fall of 1897, or while the events narrated in the preceding chapters were occurring, Joe and I did what we could on our Klondike claim, much time being spent in preparations for drifting the coming winter. Our spring cleanup, while not large, because we had been unable to work as extensively as others, and because we had poor luck in finding the pay-streak and were compelled to sink several holes before striking rich dirt, was still good enough to provide us with a comfortable amount of gold dust. While only the large fortunes suddenly amassed by the few who had worked large fractions of their claims attracted attention, we nevertheless congratulated ourselves upon our good fortune, knowing that our money was in the ground and could be taken out, if we chose, in the winter. When we returned from our somewhat unpleasant trip to the Indian River district, we at once became aware of the situation as to the food supply in Dawson, and, as we had neglected to lay in provisions early, we realized that our hopes of a prosperous winter might be dashed on the ground. We hurried down to Dawson and found affairs as already described. It was impossible to secure a full stock of provisions for the winter, but any one who would leave the country could get enough for the trip. To those who insisted upon staying a little was being doled out, with the understanding that when enough time had elapsed for its consumption another batch would be sold. The possibilities of speculating in food supplies were carefully guarded against.

Joe and I reflected and consulted. We had experienced a touch of famine the previous winter when but a few people were in the Klondike, and we did not look forward with any degree of satisfaction to the possibility of something worse. It was necessary for us either to stay to hold down our claims, or to find some one who would work them on shares. It was easy enough to find among the eager newcomers men who would make such an arrangement, but as they had no provisions to depend upon, and knew scarcely anything about mining, they would be able to do little work.

It so happened at that time that the excitement over the Indian River district was at a high point, and we had a good offer for our claims there and also the claim on the Bonanza. Joe and I lit our pipes and thought. There were many points in favor of the bird in the hand.

"But there may be millions in those mines," said Joe.

"Possibly," I replied. "We don't know about that, but we do know that there's a lot of frozen muck and gravel and hard work in them. And we know, too, that by next April we might be willing to trade one of them for a hundred of flour."

We smoked and we thought a little more, and concluded to take the bird in the hand. We reckoned that when we got the money we should have about twenty-five thousand dollars apiece.

"We can afford to have poor luck for a year or two," I said to Joe.

" And I don't feel as if we were selling our birthright, for there is plenty of gold to be found in Alaska; better diggings, I'm thinking, than these British moose pastures, especially if the government con-cludes to take a large share of the profits."

The next question was whether we should go down or up the riv-er. Joe was inclined to take the former course, but as his claim in the Birch Creek district was being worked, and as we heard rumors that there was little food to be had at Circle City unless it was sledded from Fort Yukon, we decided that we would go out to the coast and in the spring bring in a big outfit. Outfits are always profitable, and we thought there was money in the scheme.

But we were in no hurry, for we wished to wait till the ice had become solid and the trail a little packed. We got together our stove, tent blankets, and other necessities for the trip, and took life easy. So many small parties had been going out that dogs were extremely scarce. The price had started at one hundred and fifty dollars, but had soon risen to two hundred dollars, and when we began to think about them, they were worth about two hundred and fifty dollars. We smoked and thought again.

With good dogs we figured that we could reach the Coast in about thirty days; without them it would take about forty under good conditions. But Alaskan travel is uncertain, with or without dogs. One thing, however, was certain; the dogs would eat up a good part of what they would draw before they reached the coast unless we made remarkably good time, so we concluded to save our money, even if we lost some time, and draw the sleds ourselves.

So one morning late in November we bade good-bye for a time to Dawson and the Klondike, and started for the coast in a blinding snowstorm. The mercury bottles were frozen solid. The river was rougher than the rocky road to Dublin. It had frozen once, then broken up and frozen again so that it was all humps and bumps, and the only way to maintain a tolerably smooth course was to cross back and forth where the way seemed to open out best. In spite of every precaution the sleds were continually overturning while we were slipping and sprawling. Parties with dogs fared even worse. The dogs could go anywhere, but the sleds followed them sometimes right side up, but more often on one side. Many sleds were broken. Soon many of the dogs had badly lacerated feet, and in some cases they were frozen, so that we were rather glad we had concluded to depend upon ourselves, though the dog teams quickly got ahead of us and others overtook us.

All the way from Dawson to the mouth of the Pelly River the river was so rough that dogs were hardly able to haul more than enough to last them to the coast, and it was hard, cold drudgery for Joe and me. In some places, the ice was piled fifteen feet high. All the way along we encountered the wrecks of boats which had been abandoned when the river closed, the parties pushing on with only barely enough to keep them alive on the trail.

We worked along slowly, and when we had gone a dozen miles it seemed as if we had gone a hundred. Men with frozen cheeks, noses, fingers, and feet were encountered, and occasionally one in a very bad fix, but we managed to get along very comfortably till we came to the Lewis River.

The current of this stream is so rapid, and the weather up to this time had been so mild, that it was only partly frozen over, and in many places it was full of rushing and crushing ice cakes. When I say mild weather I mean, of course, mild for Alaska. As a matter of fact, the mercury had not thawed for a couple of weeks. We speak of mild weather up here in the winter when it averages about fifty below zero. Wherever the ice jams were, the ice was piled in cakes as high as six-story buildings, sloping up gradually on one side and breaking off in sheer precipices on the other. It made it much easier traveling coming out than going in. The current setting down the river runs the ice in such a way that the slope is toward Dawson. In coming out the slope can be climbed first, and then the precipice can be descended, but in going in these precipices are encountered face to face.

The greatest hardships were endured here on this long stretch of country, both by those going out and by those who had bravely made the effort to reach Dawson. One could hear tales of suffering every day, but every one who was getting along fairly well had no time for the troubles of others, although in severe cases great kindliness was shown.

There was one man who had started out early in a boat and had been compelled to return to Dawson, where he secured a dog team. At the foot of Lake Laberge he slipped and fell and sprained his leg. He had plenty of provisions, but his team made poor time, and he was suffering great pain. He offered good money to those who overtook him to pull him out, but they were in too great a hurry to get out of the country themselves.

Another young man had been left at Five Finger Rapids with both feet frozen. His companions were unable to help him along to the coast, and so left him as comfortable as they could, realizing what would be his fate. He sent messages to his friends in the East, and there he was left in a little hut with no one to care for him, except such passers-by as had their sympathy touched. He was finally taken care of by a poor family. In many camps we passed men were sick, and the prospects were that they could not survive the trials of a winter in such a place, sleeping on the snow with the thermometer sometimes as low as seventy degrees below zero.

Joe and I, who, by spending a winter on the Klondike, had learned how to prepare for the cold weather and rough trails, worked our way along very well over the rough river, though in places the ice was so thin that we and others we encountered had narrow escapes from being plunged into the river. We heard of one man who, in crossing, had broken through and slid under the ice. Of course, that was the last of him in such a swift current. At Thirty Mile River it was necessary to make a portage, for the river was running too swift to freeze at all. The trail along the banks was a hard one, and we were constantly in danger of sliding off into the river.

After many trials we reached White Horse Rapids, camping on a hill near by. The traveling on the lakes was very good, but it was a hard climb up that hill. Much of the time we had to crawl on our hands and knees while dragging our sleds, and a careless move would have sent us down into the river.

When we arrived there preparations were being made to take back to Skagway a young woman who was very ill. She had been rescued from almost certain death at a camp near Lake Laberge. She had been pushing toward Dawson with a party, and, early in November, when going over the last hill at Miles Cañon, she slipped and wrenched her right knee. A stretcher was made for her and the party pushed on to Lake Laberge, where they finally made camp, but the limb, without medical attendance, grew rapidly worse, and she succumbed to a low rheumatic fever. Her life was despaired of. Finally, she was sent back to a camp at the White Horse Rapids, where a doctor was at last found who put the knee in a plaster cast. After a time she started for Skagway lashed to a sled drawn by five dogs — a ride of one hundred and eighty-five miles, over hills and down valleys, and through blizzards!

A little incident of the trail! A little chapter in the history of gold seeking in Alaska!

Another true story of the Dyea trail is that of the Indian mother who was found kneeling in the snow, bared almost to the skin and frozen stiff. But in her rigid arms, wrapped in fold upon fold of thick furs, she held a little child, warm and safe. The mother had given her life for her child — only a poor Indian woman, but with as fine an instinct of protective motherhood as that exemplified by any of a superior race.

As we were lying on a pile of boughs in our tent that night, with our wet feet shoved up near the red hot stove, Joe said, "William, a fellow's life ain't worth much till he gets out of a place like this."
I gave him a quick glance to see if he were looking well, and saw that he was, and, as he was always sober-minded, I thought nothing more about his remark.

"You know what you told me when we arranged in Colorado to come to Alaska" I said.

"Yes, it takes grit, but we have made pretty well for two years roughing it, and I was thinking if I got out of here I would not be fool enough to return. Colorado is good enough for me. You too. We've got a snug sum, and what we need now is to get it out with our lives."

He said no more and we were soon asleep. The next day we pushed on toward the cañon. All the way along the rapid river there were open places from which a fine mist came, which quickly settled as frost upon everything. It was the most picturesque spot I ever saw. The rapids were inspiring in their grandness, seething and rushing along between fantastically shaped ice that had gathered along the banks. Over this ice we made our way carefully, though not without some fear that it would break with us and that we should be whirled off down the boiling stream, but after about three miles of it we came safely to the cañon.

"There's where I sailed out on the bottom of the *Tar Stater*," I said to Joe, as we looked up between the bluffs.

"Well, things did look blue that day, didn't they? But the question now is, which course shall we take here?"

There were two routes which we could take. One led up a hill about a hundred feet high and almost as steep as the side of a barn, and then along the top of the bluff to the other end. The other was through the cañon on the ice which had formed along the edge of the rocks. The first meant packing on our backs most of the stuff we had, and in the condition of the trail it would take all day to do it. By taking the latter course we could go through in a few minutes — if the ice would hold. We saw by the tracks that numerous dog teams had already gone through, and there seemed no reason why we should not at least make the attempt.

So we started in. The waters were roaring with that thunder tone which brought vividly back to me my four minutes trip of a few months before, and along the walls was an uneven shelf of ice which the dashing spray had formed. It seemed sufficiently wide and strong at first, but it gradually narrowed and at times brought us very near the angry water. Joe was ahead and picking his way very carefully. Finally, he came to a place where the shelf of ice was very slanting and he stepped to the outside edge so as to push the sled along and steady it, to prevent it from sliding into the water.

I was preparing to do the same thing when I heard a sharp cry from Joe, and, looking up, I saw him slip, then slide over the edge of the shelf into the raging rapids. His hand clutched the rope of the sled, and, quick as a flash, I sprang forward to catch it. But it was too late. Over went the sled into the misty foam and sank at once, for it was heavily loaded.

As I stood almost rigid with fright I saw Joe struggling bravely in the waters, but being swept rapidly down, and I knew he was no swimmer. I started and ran, but just then he was drawn under the ice shelf, and that was the last I saw of Joe. The whole thing was over almost in an instant.

Overpowered with horror and grief, I dropped down upon the ice in the midst of that roaring cañon and cried like a child.

Poor Joe! He was a brave, good, generous fellow, with a heart strong, yet tender. How he had worked and suffered to save my life that wild night on Indian River! And now he was taken away from me so quickly that I could not even throw out a helping hand. Fate had marked that cañon as a fatal place for Joe and me. We had for years worked together, suffered together, and helped each other, always without any real disagreements. And that awful cañon had swallowed him almost in an instant; and I could not even hope to find his poor body to raise over it in that wild region some rude memorial to a noble friend.

Poor Joe! Just as he had with strenuous effort wrested a little fortune from the unfriendly soil, and was hopefully looking forward to a life of happier conditions under a more genial sun, he was snatched away by Death, — dragged down to an icy grave where the wild waters lash themselves in a continual fury and their savage tumult is unceasing. And the precious dust, for which he had risked and endured so much — that too, had become the prey of that awful, insatiate force that has claimed many a life, and waits to claim yet more.

I sat for a long time bewildered, mourning with all my heart for the poor fellow, and then walked back to my sled, which had kept safely to the shelf. Then for the first time I realized my own serious predicament. I was left with the provisions, but with no tent, no stove, no cooking utensils, and only two blankets. I was tempted to jump into the rapids and follow Joe, for I knew I should freeze unless I could fall in with another party who could give me shelter and warmth. I decided to push on through the cañon, realizing that

I should not be much worse off if I also made a misstep and fell in.

That was a sad and lonely journey for me through those mountain gorges. I stopped for nothing, not even lunch, for I had nothing with which to build a fire, as I had no dry splinters. In the afternoon a terrific snowstorm came on and fell so rapidly that it soon obliterated the trail. To go on meant certain death; to attempt to camp in that storm with but two blankets to protect me meant, probably, the same thing. But the latter course offered the only chance of safety. So, as I slowly waded along, I looked about for a sheltered spot. Turning the edge of a mountain which came down to the winding river I uttered a cry of joy. There, in a nook, was a little tent half buried in snow. I hurried on, and when near, shouted loudly, but no one appeared. Opening the tent, a breath of warm air met me. Crouching close to a hot stove was a man who looked weak and sick. On a pile of boughs was another man looking still weaker and sicker.

"Got any grub?" said the man at the stove, in a husky voice, looking up to me with eager eyes.

"Too much," I said. "I want a fire and a tent."

"Wake up, Jim! Wake up! Something to eat!" He said, rousing the other man.

They had lost their provisions a long ways down the river, and had been passed along from camp to camp with just enough food to last them, but one of them had frozen the soles of his feet and for a whole day they had been camped there with nothing to eat.

"I began to think I should have to kill one of the dogs and eat him," said one of the men, after we had feasted.

"Dogs? I saw no dogs about."

"Wait a minute."

We mixed up some flour and bacon and stepped out to where the snow was drifting ever deeper and deeper. Kicking about in some little mounds in the drifted snow we found three dogs, sleeping as peacefully and snugly as possible. But how they ate! And then they lay down and let the snowdrift over them again.

The next day we pushed on rapidly, for Jim's feet were better, though still painful. I knew we must make good time if my provisions lasted three men and three dogs over the pass. But we had fair weather till we reached the summit, which we crossed in the teeth of a blizzard.

While we were at Sheep Camp there was a bad accident on the summit which we had just safely crossed. The blizzard was still raging, and as a party of coast-bound miners were coming over, an avalanche came thundering down the mountain side above the narrow defile through which the miners pass. It covered a large section of the new tramway, and several sleds and tons of provisions were a total loss. On the other side a glacier broke away, and rushed down with terrific force, burying two sleds and a part of the outfit of two men. We reached Dyea without further adventures. It was a sad journey. And as I stood on the deck of the steamer, looking back on those somber shores and frowning summits, my thoughts were of my lost friend and his tragic death.

The Law of the Yukon
Robert Service

This is the law of the Yukon,
   and ever she makes it plain:
"Send not your foolish and feeble;
   send me your strong and your sane —
Strong for the red rage of battle;
   sane, for I harry them sore;
Send me men girt for the combat,
   men who are grit to the core;
Swift as the panther in triumph,
   fierce as the bear in defeat,
Sired of a bulldog parent,
   steeled in the furnace heat.

"Send me the best of your breeding,
   lend me your chosen ones;
Them will I take to my bosom,
   them will I call my sons;
Them will I gild with my treasure,
   them will I glut with my meat;
But the others — the misfits, the failures —
   I trample them under my feet.
Dissolute, damned and despairful,
   crippled and palsied and slain,
Ye would send me the spawn of your gutters —
   Go! take back your spawn again!

"Wild and wide are my borders,
   stern as death is my sway;
From my ruthless throne I have ruled alone
   for a million years and a day;
Hugging my mighty treasure,

waiting for man to come,
Till he swept like a turbid torrent,
   after him swept — the scum.
The pallid pimp of the dead-line,
   the enervate of the pen,
One by one I weeded them out,
   for all that I sought was — Men.

"One by one I dismayed them,
   frighting them sore with my glooms;
One by one I betrayed them
   unto my manifold dooms.
Drowned them like rats in my rivers,
   starved them like curs on my plains,
Rotted the flesh that was left them,
   poisoned the blood in their veins;
Burst with my winter upon them,
   searing forever their sight,
Lashed them with fungus-white faces,
   whimpering wild in the night;

"Staggering blind through the storm-whirl,
   stumbling mad through the snow,
Frozen stiff in the ice-pack,
   brittle and bent like a bow;
Featureless, formless, forsaken,
   scented by wolves in their flight,
Left for the wind to make music,
   through ribs that are glittering white;
Gnawing the black crust of failure,
   searching the pit of despair,
Crooking the toe in the trigger,
   trying to patter a prayer;

"Going outside with an escort,
   raving with lips all afoam,
Writing a cheque for a million,
   driveling feebly of home;
Lost like a louse in the burning...
   or else in the tented town
Seeking a drunkard's solace,
   sinking and sinking down;
Steeped in the slime at the bottom,
   dead to a decent world,
Lost 'mid the human flotsam,
   far on the frontier hurled;

"In the camp at the bend of the river,
   with its dozen saloons aglare,
Its gambling dens ariot,
   its gramophones all ablare;
Crimped with the crimes of a city,
   sin-ridden and bridled with lies,
In the hush of my mountained vastness,
   in the flush of my midnight skies.
Plague-spots, yet tools of my purpose,
   so natheless I suffer them thrive,
Crushing my Weak in their clutches,
   that only my Strong may survive.

"But the others, the men of my mettle,
   the men who would 'stablish my fame
Unto its ultimate issue,
   winning me honor, not shame;
Searching my uttermost valleys,
   fighting each step as they go.
Shooting the wrath of my rapids,
   scaling my ramparts of snow;
Ripping the guts of my mountains,
   looting the beds of my creeks,

Them will I take to my bosom,
  and speak as a mother speaks.
"I am the land that listens,
  I am the land that broods;
Steeped in eternal beauty,
  crystalline waters and woods.
Long have I waited lonely,
  shunned as a thing accurst,
Monstrous, moody, pathetic,
  the last of the lands and the first;
Visioning campfires at twilight,
  sad with a longing forlorn,
Feeling my womb o'er-pregnant
  with the seed of cities unborn.

"Wild and wide are my borders,
  stern as death is my sway,
And I wait for the men who will win me —
  and I will not be won in a day;
And I will not be won by weaklings,
  subtle, suave and mild,
But by men with the hearts of Vikings,
  and the simple faith of a child;
Desperate, strong and resistless,
  unthrottled by fear or defeat,
Them will I gild with my treasure,
  them will I glut with my meat.

"Loftly I stand from each sister land,
  patient and wearily wise,
With the weight of a world of sadness
  in my quiet, passionless eyes;
Dreaming alone of a people,
  dreaming alone of a day,
When men shall not rape my riches,
  and curse me and go away;

Making a bawd of my bounty,
   fouling the hand that gave —
Till I rise in my wrath and I sweep on their path
   and I stamp them into a grave;

"Dreaming of men who will bless me,
   of women esteeming me good,
Of children born in my borders
   of radiant motherhood,
Of cities leaping to stature,
   of fame like a flag unfurled,
As I pour the tide of my riches
   in the eager lap of the world."

This is the Law of the Yukon,
   that only the Strong shall thrive;
That surely the Weak shall perish,
   and only the Fit survive.
Dissolute, damned and despairful,
   crippled and palsied and slain,
This is the Will of the Yukon —
   Lo, how she makes it plain!

From Dawson to the Sea
Jack London

It was well into June when we cast off the boat's painter, and, with the last good-byes ringing in our ears, began the 2,000-mile journey down the Yukon to St. Michael. As the six-mile current took us briskly in tow, we turned about for a final glimpse of Dawson — dreary, desolate Dawson, built in a swamp, flooded to the second story, populated by dogs, mosquitoes, and gold-seekers. Our friends attempted a half-hearted cheer, and filled the air with messages for those at home.

Our boat was homemade, weak-kneed and leaky, but in thorough harmony with the wilderness we were traversing. A smooth and polished creation of the boat-builder's art might have been more beautiful, but we were quite agreed that it would have been less comfortable and a positive discord to our rough-hewn environment. In the bow was the woodshed, while amidships, built of pine boughs and blankets, was the bedchamber. Then came the rower's bench, and, jammed between this and the steersman, was our snug little kitchen. It was a veritable home, and we had little need of going ashore, save out of curiosity or to lay in a fresh supply of firewood.

The three of us had sworn to make of this a pleasure trip, in which all labor was to be performed by gravitation, and all profit reaped by ourselves. And what a profit it was to us who had been accustomed to pack great loads on our backs or drag all day at the sleds for a paltry 25 or 30 miles. We now hunted, played cards, smoked, ate and slept, sure of our six miles an hour, of our 144 a day.

Scarcely pausing at the deserted mining camp of Forty Mile or at Fort Cudahy, we arrived at Eagle City, the first town on the American side of the boundary. What with the strange actions and heavy exactions of the Northwest Territory officials, we gave vent to a most excessive enthusiasm on once more treading the soil of Uncle Sam. The inhabitants, while waiting for some steamer to bring them food, were engaged in bucking a faro layout. But they were boomers, halting the game in a vain attempt to sell us corner lots.

Three hundred miles below Dawson we encountered Circle City, the largest camp on the Yukon previous to the Klondike discoveries, and so named because of its proximity to the Arctic Circle. It lay on the edge of the great Yukon Flats, a dismal domain, about which little is known. The Flats are a vast area of low country, extending for hundreds of miles in every direction, into which the Yukon plunges and is practically lost. The river, hitherto flowing between mountains, rugged and sternly outlined, with few islands on its breast, now begins its heartbreaking dividing and subdividing. One finds himself in a gigantic puzzle, consisting of thousands of miles of territory, and cut up into countless myriads of islands and channels. Men have been known to lose their way and wander for weeks in this perplexing maze. Great "blind" sloughs, on every hand, lie in wait for the unwary. And most exasperating it is to labor several score of miles into one of these, to find that it is "blind" (has no outlet) and that you must retrace your steps. The islands are well wooded, but, having also been well flooded, are miserable to land upon. The region is one of the greatest nesting grounds in the world, abounding with all kinds of ducks, brant, geese, and swans. The adventurer who faces this soggy wilderness of water, mud, dank vegetation and mosquitoes, does not care to linger by the way, but, with an intense longing and exceeding haste, keeps to the largest channels and swiftest currents.

Eighty-five miles within the Flats, where the Yukon crosses the Arctic Circle and makes its magnificent bend to the west and south, and the Porcupine threads the lacustrine wilderness and enters from the east, we landed at the old Hudson Bay Company post of Fort Yukon. The North American Trading and Transportation and the Alaska Commercial companies' coaches are located here, also an Indian village. During the winter, while Dawson was on the ragged edge of famine, these caches were stocked to overflowing; yet it was impossible to sled the provisions such a distance up the river, while the steamers had found it equally impossible to get up before navigation closed.

The steamer *Bella*, a year late, was industriously loading up. It was a peculiar scene of animation and excitement. Four o'clock in the morning, under the Arctic Circle, yet the sun was high in the heavens and it was already uncomfortably warm. It seemed more like some festival day at 3 o'clock in the afternoon. All was gaiety, noise, and laughter. The bucks were skylarking or flirting with the maidens; the older squaws were gossiping in bunches, while the young ones shrank and giggled in the corners. The children played or squabbled, and the babies rolled in the muck with the tawny wolf dogs. Fantastic forms, dimly outlined, flitted to and fro, surged together, eddied, parted, in the smoke-laden atmosphere. Only by nosing and poking about could one see anything; for the reeking smoke rose from untold smudges, bringing grief to the mosquito, tears to the soft eyes of the white men and giving to the whole affair a mysterious air of unreality.

Through all this portion of the trip it was hard to realize our far-northerly latitude. It was more like an enchanted land, teeming with paradoxes. For instance, gasping for breath in the noonday heat and sweltering in a tropic temperature under Arctic skies or panting on top of the blankets at midnight, the red-disked sun poised like a ball of blood above the northern horizon. And the strange beauty and charm of the noonday nights — drifting, always drifting with the stream. Now slipping down a narrow channel where the wooded shores seem to meet overhead; now flashing into the open, where a thousand streams converge and form a mighty river; and again the diverging courses, the tiny channel, the overhanging forest, the smell of the land and the damp warmth of the vegetation. And above all, the hum of life, bursting into sudden gushes of song, slowly swelling to a great, dull roar of satisfaction or dying away into sweetly cadenced silence. Not a sound as we round the tail of a bar, disturbing a solitary crane from his ghostly reveries. A partridge drums in the forest, a moose lunges noisily as it takes to the water, and again silence. Then an owl hoots from some gloomy recess or a raven croaks gutturally overhead. Suddenly, the wild cry of a loon sweeps across a glassy stretch of river, awakening myriad answers. The robins open their full, rich throats and the woods burst into music. The tree squirrels play a dozen instruments at once, while the blackbirds sing shrill choruses to the sharp-marked time of the woodpecker. The pure treble of the songbirds is accompanied by the steady boom boom of the partridge, till all is lost in the general pandemonium. Then the wild fowl of the swamp join the quick crescendo, and the finale, swelled to bursting, slowly dies away. A killdeer calls timidly to its mate, and silence falls.

After 200 miles of the Flats, we made Minook, the principal mining camp on the Lower River. It has since received the less
euphemistic name of Rampart City. While the news of Dawson was
by no means fresh, the men of the Lower River had had none all
winter; so we landed amid a bombardment of queries. They were
mostly perturbed over the war, the Thanksgiving football game, and
the execution of Durant. True to Northland tradition, we expanded items into chapters, yet failed utterly in satisfying their unholy lust
for news.

Running the rapids below Minook, where the Yukon at some early period cut its way through the Rampart Mountains, we made
Tanana station. Here also was the Indian town of Nuklukyeto, while
several miles below stood the old mission of St. James. Great was the
merrymaking as we arrived in the wee, small hours. The spring run
of salmon was expected at any moment, and the mission, Tanana and
Tozikakats were all assembled, to say nothing of the great sprinkling
contributed by the several hundred miles of Yukon on either side of
the station. We landed our heavy craft amid the litter of flimsy bark
canoes which lined the bank, and found ourselves in the great fishing camp. Picking our steps among the tents and wading through
the sprawling babies and fighting dogs, we made our way to a large
log structure where a dance was in progress. After much pushing and
shoving, we forced an entrance through the swarming children. The
long, low room was literally packed with dancers. There was no
light, no ventilation, save through the crowded doorway, and, in the
semi-darkness, strapping bucks and wild-eyed squaws sweated,
howled, and reveled in a dance which defies description. With the
peculiar elation of the traveler who scales the virgin peak, we prepared to enjoy the novelty of the situation; but, imagine our disappointment on discovering that even here 1,000 miles beyond the
uttermost bounds of civilization, the adventurous white man already
had penetrated. In the crowded room, dizzy with heat and the smell
of bodies, we at last discerned the fair-bronzed skin, the blue eyes,
and the blond mustache of the ubiquitous Anglo-Saxon. A glance
demonstrated how thoroughly at home he was.

One hundred miles below Nuklukyeto, our midnight watch was
beguiled by a wild chant, which rose and fell uncannily as it float-

ed across the water. An hour later we rounded a bend and landed at a fishing village, so engrossed in its religious rites that our arrival was unnoted. Climbing the bank, we came full upon the weird scene. It brought us back to the orgies of the cavemen and more closely in touch with our common ancestor, probably arboreal, which Mr. Darwin has so fittingly described. Several score of bucks were giving tongue to unwritten music, evidently born when the world was very young, and still apulse with the spirit of primeval man. Urged on by the chief medicine man, the women had abandoned themselves to the religious ecstasy, their raven hair unbound and falling to their hips, while their bodies were swaying and undulating to the swing of the song.

All through the interior, save in the sheltered nooks and on the northern slopes of the loftier peaks, the snow had quite disappeared by the middle of June. But from Tozikakat it began to grow more plentiful, till at Koyokuk, even the southern exposure was no longer bare — a sign that we were approaching the coast, or rather, the coast climate, for we were still 700 miles above the mouth of the river. It is naturally thus with a marine climate, where, because of the great body of water, the heat is neither absorbed nor radiated as rapidly as in the interior. Hence, the winters are much colder and the summers equally warmer at Dawson than at St. Michael. Along the shores of Bering Sea, even a month after the sun has passed its northern solstice, great bodies of snow are to be found lying at the water's edge.

At Nulato, 650 miles above the mouth, we found two small steamers fitting out and extensive preparations being made for the exploration of the Koyokuk, which is looked upon as the coming Alaskan Klondike. We were just in time for service at the Roman Catholic mission, and, strange it was, gazing upon the finely chiseled features of the be-moccasined, black-stoled priest, and listening to the strange unison of the shrill voices of the Indian women and the deep basses of the fathers. Father Monroe, a cultured, and as rumor puts it, a very wealthy Frenchman, has devoted his life to the cause of the missions, and for five long years has labored zealously at Nulato. The Indians are always more energetic, thrifty, and of better appearance at the missions than elsewhere, though Christianity seems never to get a really deep hold on them. Several of my sou-

venirs will testify to the readiness with which they will trade a cru-
cifix for an old pack of cards.

It has been a very early spring, and the breaking of the Yukon was
accompanied by the greatest high-water known for years. From
Dawson to Kutlik, every station and long-established village had
been severely flooded, many being washed away. If signs are to be
trusted, the ice-run for the last 500 miles of river must have been
terrific. Many portions of the mainland and whole islands had been
swept clear of the timber which always clusters thickly in the bot-
toms. The large trees are uprooted or literally gnawed in two by the
grinding ice, while the smaller ones bend before it and are rubbed
clean of bark, reminding one of well-picked bones on some endless
battlefield.

Game and fish were quite abundant the whole length of the river, and every camp had a fresh bearskin or so stretched on the dry-
ing frames. While we did much of our own hunting, we did not
waste time in gathering eggs or fishing, preferring to trade for such
staples. However, we were usually disappointed in the eggs, not rel-
ishing the embryonic diet of ducks and geese which the natives so
delight inn. But the fish were excellent, especially the salmon. Oh,
you who pay big for the silver salmon of the fish market and then
say it is good, come north and buy a great king salmon, weighing
from 40 to 50 pounds of clean meat, for a tin cup or so of flour. They
are to be found in the pink of condition in the icy waters of the
Yukon, cold, firm-fleshed and, above all, delicious. But it takes one
quite a time to learn to trade with the Indians. He must have the
foresight of Joseph and the patience of Job, else will he be mulcted
as the Gentile should be. The practiced hand endeavors to exhibit a
well-disguised desire for the article he does not wish, and but ordinary interest in that which he is after. The native will then elevate
the price of the former and correspondingly depress that of the latter. When he has thus brought the thing you wish absurdly low, snap
it quick and pay on the spot. He will be chagrined, but a bargain's
a bargain.

The hunting we could not forego, though the shotgun was old and
decrepit, and one trigger persisted in discharging both barrels. Very
pleasant it was during midnight lookouts, listening to the comrades
snoring beneath the mosquito tent, drifting along the low-flooded

banks, watching the sun above the northern horizon and dropping the startled wild fowl as they rose from the river.

By the time we arrived at Anvik, 600 miles from the mouth, we began to realize the mighty river we were voyaging on. At Fort Yukon, 1300 miles from the mouth, it is 8 miles wide; at the Koyokuk it narrows to 2 or 3 miles, and from Koserefski it maintains a width of from 8 to 10 miles, till it is lost in the Great Delta, where its southern and northern mouths are over 80 miles apart. But at Anvik it is 40 miles wide, with a spring rise of from 30 to 40 feet. This great width is due to a division which makes possible one of the largest inland islands of the world — an island that is not even named.

A totally different native population is encountered from Anvik to the sea. The clean-limbed stalwart Indians disappear, being replaced by the Malemutes, who are a sort of mongrel cross of Thlinket and Esquimau. Poverty-stricken, with little energy and no ambition, they have not furnished much inducement to the white traders; hence, they continue to exist on a straight fish and meat diet, washed down with incalculable quantities of vile-smelling seal oil. Their houses are merely holes in the ground, shored with driftwood timbers. In the center of this they build an open fire, the smoke of which escapes through a vent hole in the roof. In the wintertime, the men, women and children crowd into these burrows like sardines. The sanitary, social, and moral conditions may be conjectured. They have quite a reverence for their dead, however; their burial places being neat, clean, and pleasing to the eye. Rough palings surround the graves, which are usually covered with a rain shed. Fantastic designs are often painted upon them by the means of soot and seal oil. Occasionally, a curiously carved totem pole is raised; but, by the crosses the great majority rest in the consecrated ground of the Catholic Church. It is hard to say what becomes of the Protestant converts, but the more impressive ritual of the Catholic service, opposed to the bare, Puritanical mode of Protestant worship, and so pregnant with mysticism to the barbaric mind, may perhaps explain it.

From the Mission of the Holy Cross to the Russian Mission of Icogmute, we found the mountains dwindling sadly, and at Andrefsky we bade farewell to the last barren hills and plunged into the dismal solitude of the Great Delta of the Yukon. It was a repetition of the Flats, but fraught with more serious consequences. A mistake in this uncharted wilderness and one would blunder into the Southern Channel, wandering no man knows whither, till he emerged, without guide or landmark, on the bleak coast of Bering Sea. Disdaining Malemute guides, we were two days in traveling these 120 miles. We gave vent to much foolish enthusiasm when we felt the first pulse of the tide; and when in Kutlik we slept in sight of open sea, deemed ourselves to be nearly home.

The 80-mile run up the coast was full of excitement. As we skirted dangerous Point Romanoff, we picked up a Jesuit priest who was having a hard time in the surf. And for all the cloth he was a jolly fellow, pulling an oar, smoking a pipe or telling a tale with the next one. He was an illustration of the many strange types to be found in the Northland. An Italian by blood, a Frenchman by birth, a Spaniard by education and an American by residence, he was a marvelous scholar and his whole life was one continuous romance; but sworn to the oaths of his order, he had sacrificed twelve prime years of his life in bleak Alaska, and in all things, even to reducing the Inuit language to a grammar, was happy.

Our last taste of Bering Sea was a fitting close to the trip. Midnight found us wallowing in the sea, a rocky coast to lee-ward and a dirty sky to windward, with splutters of rain and wind squalls which soon developed into a gale. Removing the sprit and bagging the after-leech, we shortened to storm canvas and ran before it, reaching the harbor of St. Michael just 21 days from the time we cast off the lines at Dawson.

Disaster at Nome
Rex Beach

The following summer news of the Klondike gold discovery threw the country into a raging fever. I read the highly imaginative accounts of buried riches in the Yukon, bought a map and read up on the rules of gold mining as I had read up on law and football.

I reasoned thus: at the rate I was going it would require quite a while to crash the Supreme court, and if in the meantime I had to depend upon athletics to keep body and soul together I'd be too stiff and waterlogged to sit on the bench, so why not take a year out, scurry up to Alaska and excavate a fortune? If necessary I could well afford to spend a couple of years at it; I'd still be back by the time I was old enough to vote. Hardship and privation were nothing to worry about. Freezing is a far pleasanter death than drowning, the sensations of which are familiar to any water-polo player, and as for hunger, I was starved most of the time anyhow.

I worried a grubstake from my indulgent brothers, bought a fur-lined sleeping bag, rifle, a dogskin suit, and a mandolin. With these I left Chicago between sun and sun.

I had that mandolin with me two years later when an itinerant steam whaler landed me back in Seattle. Music was scarce on the Yukon, it had enabled me to pick up a bit of refreshment now and then, playing for squaw dances. I was all but broke and, having slept, during the homeward voyage, wherever there was room to curl up, I was as lousy as a pet coon. I had subsisted for the three weeks that voyage consumed on canned salmon, and to this day when it is served I emit faint, incoherent sounds of loathing.

That winter I again attended law school but my blood chemistry had change. It was the salmon in me, no doubt; an upstream urge driving me back to the spawning grounds. Anyhow I no longer had the desire to wear a Supreme Court parka.

About the time I left the North, some inexperienced miners at Nome discovered a pay streak on the beach, laid down by the restless surf of Behring Sea. With the crudest of hand appliances a lot of money had been taken out in a few short weeks, and unlike other deposits of gold, this one lay along a narrow no man's land below high-tide line where the mining laws did not apply and which was open to everybody.

I sounded like a simple matter to devise special machinery to wash those sands by the ton instead of by the shovelful and I interested some people in financing such an attempt. We engaged an engineer to design a contraption and shipped it west in time for me to catch the first boat north in the spring.

So sensational were the reports of this new Golconda that another rush occurred as spectacular in its way as the Klondike stampede two years before. Every available derelict was chartered and inside of ten days after the ice went out of Behring Sea, Nome grew from a town of three to thirty thousand. Of that number I was one.

When that hysterical army was dumped ashore together with mountains of freight, fuel, mine supplies and building materials, the chaos can be imagined. Nome itself, a thin row of saloons, dugouts and canvas shelters, lay like a wagon track between the surf and a treeless, spongy tundra that ran back to a low range of inhospitable hills. Into the wet moss and mud one's boots sank to the knees; aside from the sandy beach there was not a dry place to stand and, of course, nobody had time to sit down.

That was an exciting show. There was no law to speak of: bickerings and quarrels went on everywhere and a person could pick the sort of fight he preferred. An occasional gun battle filled one with a not unpleasant sense of insecurity inasmuch as the bystanders usually suffered.

I was but one of many who had brought mechanical equipment with which to work the beach sands, and the task of assembling, transporting and setting it up in the midst of that confusion was pretty good training in self-reliance and ingenuity. By the time I had pre-empted a location a few miles from town, hired a crew and got the machinery running, I considered myself something of a rough-and-tumble executive.

That beach pay streak lay close to the surface and it had already been worked over with rocker and sluice box down to low-tide line; our intention was to reach out into the surf with our dredges and sand suckers and rob the ocean bed of its virgin wealth. There were scores of different devices but the only suckers that really worked were the owners.

Presumably there was, and still is, considerable gold lying close in to the Nome shore but nobody is certain, for human ingenuity has never been equal to the task of recovering it.

My hired men shrank from getting wet and they shrieked like Vassar girls when that cold surf engulfed them, so for weeks I battled with it practically single-handed. It beat upon me as if I were the coast of Maine. Constant immersion turned me blue; I took on the coloring of a tuna and got so I darted at schools of bait.

When at last I began to suspect that human strength was too puny to combat the resistless forces of Nature she removed all possible doubt by staging an exhibition on the grand scale. A gale blew up and steadily increased its fury for three days, littering the golden sands of Nome with the wreckage of those costly dredging machines.

I took what gold I had saved in the sluices and melted it into a button about the size of a Chicago Athletic Association Swimming medal. It weighed twenty-five dollars, and so ended that mining operation. It would have been a more brilliant success, of course, had the price of gold been as high then as it is now but a bald-headed guy stole the button anyhow, so what the heck?

Having paid off the crew I took stock of my possessions and found they consisted of a blue-flame oil burner, a centrifugal pump, some six-inch rubber hose, and a case of canned cherries. Not even among the odds and ends could I find anything to use for money. Nor were there any jobs to he had, for out of the thirty thousand newcomers who had arrived in June approximately twenty-nine thousand were in a fix as bad as mine. Furthermore I never had been a good mandolin player. Winter was approaching; obviously it was time to use my wits, if such there were.

Largely by chance I stumbled upon a mining claim that was for sale. It looked promising and I found a purchaser for it, which was something of a miracle, then using much the same technique I had employed on "Big Bill" Thompson, I talked my way into partnership with the new owner. We had a bit of luck and few weeks later I refused an offer for thirty thousand dollars for my interest in the property.

Those were crowded, colorful years and it was fun to experiment with life, trying a little of this with a pinch of that to see how it would taste. Eventually, however, I began to suspect that I lacked not only what it took to be a lawyer but also what it required to be a miner. Perseverance? N-no! I was willing to persevere at anything that interested me sufficiently to make the sacrifice: I simply hadn't found the thing I enjoyed doing more than a few times hand running. Meanwhile five years had galloped past leaving me an old man of twenty-four. I was fairly well preserved but the autumn was near, soon I would be in the sere and yellow thirties. Life is real, life is earnest and the gravy is its goal! Obviously it was high time to wave bye-bye to the gay frontier and head home. This I did.

Also available from Wolf Creek Books

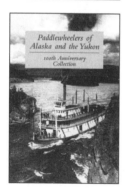
Visit us at:
www.wolfcreek.ca